COLOR BLOCK KNITS

COLOR BLOCK
KNITS

35 self-striping designs knitted with cake yarns and color wheels

NICKI TRENCH

CICO BOOKS
LONDON NEW YORK

Published in 2019 by CICO Books
An imprint of Ryland Peters & Small Ltd
20–21 Jockey's Fields, London WC1R 4BW
341 E 116th St, New York, NY 10029

www.rylandpeters.com

10 9 8 7 6 5 4 3 2 1

ISBN: 978 1 78249 712 7

Printed in China

Editor: Marie Clayton
Pattern checkers: Jane Czaja and
Marilyn Wilson
Designer: Alison Fenton
Photographer: James Gardiner
Stylist: Nel Haynes
Illustrator: Stephen Dew

Art director: Sally Powell
Production controller: David Hearn
Publishing manager: Penny Craig
Publisher: Cindy Richards

contents

introduction

Color block knitting is like magic: you never know what's coming next! The delight is in the surprise as you see the colors ebb and flow as you knit. There are only a few yarn ends to sew in—and that's just when your ball runs out, because the color changes are spun into each ball of yarn.

This type of yarn works best with projects that use a whole ball, to really get the full benefit of the color changes. And there is no need for too many fancy textured stitches, because the colors speak for themselves. However, in this collection, just to mix it up a bit, we not only have some simple stockinette (stocking) stitch and garter stitch projects (Mini Dress on page 70, Bunny Baby Hat on page 108, and Garter Stitch Blanket on page 60), but I've also chosen some textured stitches that show the colors up really well, such as on the Bobble Blanket on page 46, Diamonds Baby Blanket on page 101, and the Lace Shawl on page 84.

There are projects for all levels of knitters, from simple Leg Warmers (page 24) and Arm Warmers (page 34), to the more challenging Lace Cardigan (page 64) or Cable Cowl (page 10). We also have a good range of projects, from lovely baby and toddler garments and animal lovies to throw pillows (cushions), a hot water bottle cover, and hats and scarves. We even have a really fabulous roll-neck cable sweater that knits up to a man's size (page 76).

If you are fazed by any of the techniques, there is a great illustrated technique section that will guide you through some basic stitches and joining techniques, as well as how to make mini pompoms and tassels.

The projects have been knitted on various straight, circular, or double-pointed needles. I tend to use wooden knitting needles because I find they are more forgiving than the metal ones, but use the needles you're used to and feel most comfortable with. You'll find a list of suppliers that I recommend at the back of the book, who supplied many of the materials for the projects in the book.

Sometimes colors and yarns get discontinued or maybe you can't get hold of them where you live. Don't be afraid to replace yarns with another shade, or with another color block yarn in a similar yarn weight. There is a gauge (tension) guide on nearly all of the projects, which will help you to match replacement yarns.

I really hope you get to make many of the projects in this book—wear, give, or display your color block knitting with pride and enjoy the admiration you are sure to receive!

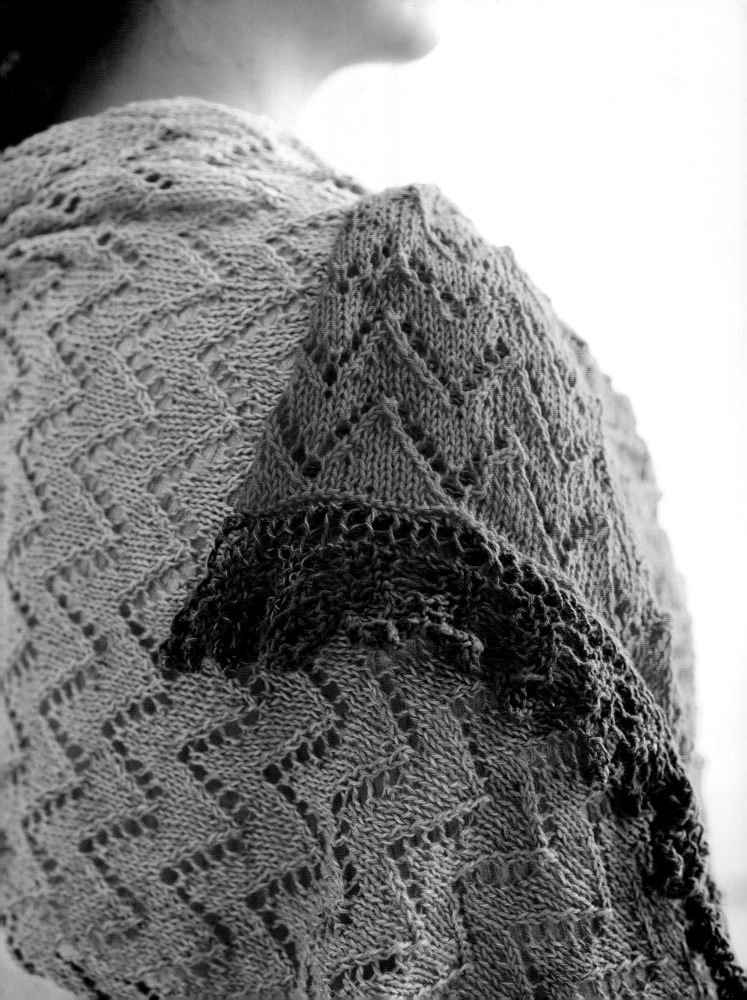

chapter 1
accessories

tip

Use a row counter to mark the 20-row pattern, crossing the cable on Rows 4 and 14.

SKILL RATING ● ● ●

MATERIALS

Caron Cakes (100% acrylic, approx. 382yds/350m per 7oz/200g ball) worsted (aran) weight yarn
  2 balls of 17010 Faerie Cake

US size 10 (6mm) knitting needles

Cable needle or double-pointed needle

Row counter

Yarn sewing needle

FINISHED MEASUREMENTS

Approx. 53½ x 7½in (136 x 19cm)

GAUGE (TENSION)

3 cables (unstretched) x 24 rows over a 5in (12.5cm) square in cable pattern, using US size 10 (6mm) needles.

ABBREVIATIONS

approx.	approximately
k	knit
p	purl
patt	pattern
rep	repeat
sl	slip
st(s)	stitch(es)
[ ]	repeat sequence between square brackets the number of times stated

cable cowl

The horizontal cables on this cowl and the colors of the Faerie Cake yarn create the impression of waves on the sea. This is a really lovely cowl to make—it's worked on straight needles and then the seams are joined at the end to create a cozy ring of cable fabric.

FOR THE COWL

Cast on 55 sts.
Row 1: K2, [k2, p8, k2, k1] 4 times, k1.
Row 2: K2, [p2, k8, p2, k1] 4 times, k1.
Row 3: Rep Row 1.
Row 4: K2, *p2, sl next 4 sts onto cable needle and hold in back, k4, k4 from cable needle, p2, k1; rep from * 3 times, k1.
Rows 5–12: Rep Rows 1 and 2 four times.
Row 13: Rep Row 1.
Row 14: K2, *p2, sl next 4 sts onto cable needle and hold in front, k4, k4 from cable needle, p2, k1; rep from * 3 times, k1.
Rows 15–20: Rep Rows 1 and 2 three times.
Rep Rows 1–20 until 300 rows are worked and cowl measures approx. 53½in (136cm).
Bind (cast) off.

FINISHING

Use mattress stitch to join the seam, matching the cables as you go. Sew in any yarn ends.

summer bag

Even in the depths of winter this bag will cheer you up; it has such a lovely beachy, seaside feel. The color changes of the yarn work out in almost equal stripes, and it has a cute textured stitch.

SKILL RATING ● ● ●

MATERIALS

Caron Simply Soft (100% acrylic, approx. 314yds/228m per 6oz/170g ball) worsted (aran) weight yarn
  1 ball of 9776 Lemonade (yellow) (A)

Caron Cupcakes (100% acrylic, approx. 243yds/223m per 3oz/85g ball) light worsted (DK) weight yarn
  4 balls of 16013 Pistachio Cup (B)

US size 6 (4mm) knitting needles

Yarn sewing needle

32 x 30in (80 x 75cm) of lining fabric

1yd (1m) of ribbon

FINISHED MEASUREMENTS

12 x 12in (30 x 30cm)

GAUGE (TENSION)

6 bobble sts x 13 bobble rows over a 4in (10cm) square, using US size 6 (4mm) needles and Caron Cupcakes yarn.

ABBREVIATIONS:

approx.	approximately
inc	increase
k	knit
p	purl
p3tog	purl 3 stitches together
patt	pattern
rep	repeat
RS	right side
st(s)	stitch(es)
WS	wrong side
[ ]	repeat sequence between square brackets the number of times stated

FOR THE BAG

The main part of the bag is knitted in one piece.

Using A, cast on 64 sts

SEED (MOSS) STITCH TOP BORDER 1

Row 1 (RS): [K1, p1] to end.
Row 2 (WS): [P1, k1] to end.
Rep these 2 rows 6 times more (14 rows).
Next row (RS): Rep Row 1 once more.
Cut A.
Next row (WS): Using B, *p3, inc 1 (purlwise); rep from * to end. *80 sts.*

BEGIN PATT ROWS

Row 1 (RS): P to end.
Row 2 (WS): *(K1, p1, k1) all in same st, p3tog; rep from * to end.
Row 3 (RS): P to end.
Row 4 (WS): *P3tog, (k1, p1, k1) all in next st; rep from * to end.
Rep patt rows 1–4 until work measures approx. 20in (50.5cm), ending on a Row 3.
Next row (WS): Using B, *p3, p2tog; rep from * to end. *64 sts.*
Cut B.

SEED (MOSS) STITCH TOP BORDER 2

Next row (RS): Using A, [k1, p1] to end.
Next row (WS): [P1, k1] to end.
Rep last two rows 6 times more.
Bind (cast) off.

FOR THE HANDLES

(make 2)
Using A, cast on 10 sts.
Row 1: [K1, p1] to end.
Row 2: [P1, k1] to end.
Rep these 2 rows until work measures approx. 20in (50.5cm).
Bind (cast) off.

FINISHING

Pin and block the bag. With RS together, sew the side seams. Turn RS out.

ADD THE LINING

Measure the knitted bag and the handles and cut out 2 lining pieces for the bag and one for each handle, allowing an extra ⅞in (2cm) all around each edge for the seam allowance. Make up the lining and line the handles as described on page 125.

Insert the lining into the bag with WS together and insert the ends of the handles between the lining and knitted pieces approx. 2in (5cm) from each edge. Cut the ribbon in half and fit one end between the lining and knitted bag in the center and pin into the bag on each side. Hand sew along the top of bag, attaching the handles and ribbon at the same time.

fingerless lace mittens

These are really delicate little lace gloves, which perfectly suit the subtle color changes of warm reds and pinks in the yarn.

MATERIALS

Schoppel Wolle Zauberball 100 (100% wool, approx. 437yds/400m per 3½oz/100g ball) light fingering (3-ply) weight yarn
  1 ball of 2166 Hot Iron

US size 1/2 (2.5mm) straight knitting needles

Set of 4 US size 1/2 (2.5mm) double-pointed needles

Yarn sewing needle

FINISHED MEASUREMENTS

Approx. 6½in (16cm) long (with rolled up edges) x 3in (7.5cm) wide (unstretched)

GAUGE (TENSION)

36 sts x 48 rows over a 4in (10cm) square in stockette (stocking) stitch, using US size 1/2 (2.5mm) needles.

ABBREVIATIONS

approx.	approximately
beg	begin
k	knit
k2tog	knit 2 stitches together
p	purl
patt	pattern
prev	previous
rep	repeat
RH	right hand
RS	right side
ssk	slip slip knit
st(s)	stitch(es)
st st	stockinette (stocking) stitch
WS	wrong side
yo	yarn over
[ ]	repeat sequence between square brackets the number of times stated

SPECIAL ABBREVIATIONS

[yo] twice: double yarnover: take yarn around the RH needle twice into position to knit next st. If next st is to be purled, yarn is brought under needle to front once more to purl position

tip

The lace pattern stitch is a multiple of 10 sts plus 4 sts.

FOR THE RIGHT MITTEN

Using US size 1/2 (2.5mm) straight needles, cast on 54 sts.
Work st st for 24 rows, approx. 2in (5cm), ending on WS row.

BEG LACE PATT

Row 1 (RS): K26, yo, ssk, *k1, k2tog, [yo] twice, ssk; rep from * to last 11 sts, k1, k2tog, yo, k8.
Row 2: P, working into front and back of every "[yo] twice" of prev row.
Row 3: K26, *k2tog, yo, k6, yo, ssk; rep from * to last 8 sts, k8.
Row 4: P.
Row 5: K27, *k2tog, yo, k4, yo, ssk, k2; rep from * to last 7 sts, k7.
Row 6: Rep Row 4.
Row 7: K28, *k2tog, yo, k2, yo, ssk, k4; rep from * to last 6 sts, k6.
Row 8: Rep Row 4.
Row 9: Rep Row 1.
Row 10: Rep Row 2.
Row 11: K29, *yo, ssk, k2tog, yo, k6; rep from * to last 5 sts, k5.
Row 12: Rep Row 4.
Row 13: K28, *yo, ssk, k2, k2tog, yo, k4; rep from * to last 6 sts, k6.
Rep 14: Rep Row 4.
Row 15: K27, *yo, ssk, k4, k2tog, yo, k2; rep from * to last 7 sts, k7.
Row 16: Rep Row 4.
Rep Rows 1–16 twice.
Work st st for 8 rows.
Bind (cast) off.

FOR THE LEFT MITTEN

Using US size 1/2 (2.5mm) straight needles, cast on 54 sts.
Work st st for 24 rows, approx. 2in (5cm), ending on WS row.

BEG LACE PATT

Row 1(RS): K8, yo, ssk, *k1, k2tog, [yo] twice, ssk; rep from * to last 29 sts, k1, k2tog, yo, k26.
Row 2: P, working into front and back of every "[yo] twice" of prev row.
Row 3: K8, *k2tog, yo, k6, yo, ssk; rep from * to last 26 sts, k26.
Row 4: P.
Row 5: K9, *k2tog, yo, k4, yo, ssk, k2; rep from * to last 25 sts, k25.
Row 6: Rep Row 4.
Row 7: K10, *k2tog, yo, k2, yo, ssk, k4; rep from * to last 24 sts, k24.
Row 8: Rep Row 4.
Row 9: Rep Row 1.
Row 10: Rep Row 2.
Row 11: K11, *yo, ssk, k2tog, yo, k6; rep from * to last 29 sts, k29.
Row 12: Rep Row 4.
Row 13: K10, *yo, ssk, k2, k2tog, yo, k4; rep from * to last 24 sts, k24.
Row 14: Rep Row 4.
Row 15: K9, *yo, ssk, k4, k2tog, yo, k2; rep from * to last 25 sts, k25.
Row 16: Rep Row 4.
Rep Rows 1–16 twice.
Work st st for 8 rows.
Bind (cast) off.

FINISHING

Pin and block each mitten.

Working on the RS, from the bottom upward, sew the seam with mattress stitch, leaving an approx. 2in (5cm) gap for the thumbhole approx. 3in (7.5cm) from the bottom edge. Rep for the second mitten.

THUMBHOLE EDGINGS

Using US size 1/2 (2.5mm) double-pointed needles, pick up and knit 36 sts evenly around thumbhole gap.
Bind (cast) off.
Using a yarn sewing needle and length of yarn, sew the last st of the thumb edging to the first st of the thumb edging.

Rep for the second mitten.

Press the mittens lightly using a damp cloth.

man's beanie hat

This is a really interesting rib stitch, which looks great when stretched out. It's simple, not too bulky, and makes a great spring or fall hat.

MATERIALS

Schoppel Wolle Gradient (100% wool, approx. 284yds/260m per 3½oz/100g ball) light worsted (DK) weight yarn
  1 ball of 1535 Stone Washed

US size 6 (4mm) circular needle, 16in (40cm) long

Set of 4 US size 6 (4mm) double-pointed needles

Stitch marker

Yarn sewing needle

FINISHED MEASUREMENTS

To fit an average-size man's head, approx. 24in (60cm) around

GAUGE (TENSION)

34 sts x 28 rows over a 4in (10cm) square in pattern unstretched, using US size 6 (4mm) needles.

ABBREVIATIONS

approx.	approximately
beg	beginning
k	knit
k2tog	knit 2 stitches together
p	purl
p2tog	purl 2 stitches together
patt	pattern
rep	repeat
st(s)	stitch(es)
[ ]	repeat sequence between square brackets the number of times stated

FOR THE HAT

Using US size 6 (4mm) circular needle, cast on 100 sts.
Join into a round, and place marker to denote beg round.
Round 1: [K4, p2, k2, p2] to end of round.
Rep Round 1 until work measures approx. 8in (20cm).
Next round: Change to US size 6 (4mm) double-pointed needles, [k2tog, k2, p2, k2, p2] around, with 3 patt reps on first needle, 4 patt reps on second needle, 3 patt reps on third needle.
Next round: [K3, p2, k2, p2] to end of round.
Next round: [K1, k2tog, p2, k2, p2] to end of round.
Next round: [K2, p2, k2, p2] to end of round.
Next round: [K2, p2tog] to end of round.
Next round: [K2, p2tog] to end of round.
Next round: [K2tog, p1] to end of round.
Next round: [K1, p1] to end of round.
Next round: [K1, p1] to end of round.
Next round: [K2tog] to end of round.
Next round: K.
Next round: [K2tog] to end of round.
Cut yarn leaving a long end, thread end through rem sts, draw up and secure.

FINISHING

Sew in all yarn ends.

loopy scarf

The looped stitch gives this scarf a lovely thick depth, so it's definitely one to wear in those colder months—and the warm shades of pink and red are perfect for brightening up winter days, too.

FOR THE BAG

Cast on 28 sts.
K 1 row.
Begin patt:
Row 1 (RS): K1, *loop st, k1; rep from * to last st, k1.
Row 2 (WS): K.
Row 3: K2, *loop st, k1; rep from * to end.
Row 4: K.
Rep Rows 1–4 until scarf measures approx. 70in (178cm), ending on a Row 2 or 4.
Bind (cast) off.

FINISHING

Sew in any loose ends.

SKILL RATING ● ● ●

MATERIALS

Caron Cakes (100% acrylic, approx. 382yds/350m per 7oz/200g ball) worsted (aran) weight yarn
 2 balls of 17004 Cherry Chip

US size 7 (4.5mm) knitting needles

Yarn sewing needle

FINISHED MEASUREMENTS

70in (178cm) long x 7in (17.5cm) wide

GAUGE (TENSION)

16 sts x 24 rows over a 4in (10cm) square in loop stitch, using US size 7 (4.5mm) needles.

ABBREVIATIONS

approx.	approximately
k	knit
patt	pattern
rep	repeat
RS	right side
st(s)	stitch(es)
WS	wrong side

SPECIAL ABBREVIATION

Loop st: loop stitch: Insert right needle into loop on left needle as if to knit st as normal. Wrap yarn around needle and bring right needle through as if knitting st, but do not slip loop off needle. Open out needles, keeping right thumb in middle, bring yarn over to front wrapping it round thumb, pass the yarn through to back between needles (yarn is wrapped around thumb). Knit st with thumb still wrapped by yarn. Release thumb from strand of yarn to create loop. Slip first st over second to secure loop (one loop stitch made)

woman's slouch hat with pompom

You can't beat a sling-it-on slouch hat. This one has a really lovely shape and is a very simple hat to work on circular or double-pointed needles. The mini pompoms add a fun decoration, and the same yarn is used for the legwarmers on pages 24–25 if you want to make a matching set.

MATERIALS

Lion Brand Amazing (53% wool, 47% acrylic, approx. 147yds/135m per 1¾oz/50g ball) worsted (aran) weight yarn
  1 ball of 212 Mauna Loa

US size 6 (4mm) circular knitting needle, 16in (40cm) long

Set of 4 US size 6 (4mm) double-pointed needles

Stitch marker

Yarn sewing needle

FINISHED MEASUREMENTS

Approx. 16in (40cm) circumference, 9in (23cm) high

GAUGE (TENSION)

20 sts x 24 rows over a 4in (10cm) square in stockinette (stocking) stitch, using US size 6 (4mm) needles.

ABBREVIATIONS

approx.	approximately
beg	beginning
cont	continue
k	knit
k2tog	knit 2 stitches together
p	purl
rem	remain
rep	repeat
st(s)	stitch(es)
[ ]	repeat sequence between square brackets the number of times stated

FOR THE HAT

Using US size 6 (4mm) circular needle, cast on 80 sts.
Join into a round, place marker to denote beg of round.
Rounds 1–12: [K1, p1] rib to end of round.
Rounds 13–47: K.

SHAPE TOP OF HAT
Round 1: *K2tog, k6; rep from * to end of round. *70 sts.*
Beg working in st st (k every round with RS facing).
Round 2: K.
Round 3: *K2tog, k5; rep from * to end of round. *60 sts.*
Round 4: K.
Round 5: *K2tog, k4; rep from * to end of round. *50 sts.*
Round 6: K.
Round 7: *K2tog, k3; rep from * to end of round. *40 sts.*
Round 8: K.
Round 9: Change to double-pointed needles during this round, *k2tog, k2; rep from * to end of round. *30 sts.*
Round 10: K.
Round 11: *K2tog, k1; rep from * to end of round. *20 sts.*
Round 12: K.
Round 13: *K2tog; rep from * to end of round. *10 sts.*
Cut yarn, leaving a long tail. Thread yarn tail through rem 10 sts on needle, removing sts from needle. Pull tail to gather top of hat.
Sew in end and leave a long tail.

FINISHING

Block and sew in any yarn ends.

Make 3 mini pompoms using the fork method (see page 126). Attach the pompoms to the top of the hat.

MATERIALS

Lion Brand Amazing (53% wool, 47% acrylic, approx. 147yds/135m per 1¾oz/50g ball) worsted (aran) weight yarn
  2 balls of 212 Mauna Loa

Set of 4 US size 8 (5mm) double-pointed needles

Yarn sewing needle

FINISHED MEASUREMENTS

Approx. 10in (25cm) circumference, 19in (48cm) long

GAUGE (TENSION)

19 sts x 25 rows over a 4in (10cm) square in stockinette (stocking) stitch, using US size 8 (5mm) needles.

ABBREVIATIONS

approx.	approximately
beg	beginning
k	knit
p	purl
st(s)	stitch(es)
st st	stockinette (stocking stitch)

leg warmers

These are a really great project for learning to knit in the round. The wool is a tweed version of colorblock yarn and these are perfect to keep legs warm in those cold, chilly months.

FOR THE LEG WARMERS

Cast on 15 sts on each of first two needles and 14 sts on third needle. Join round, place marker to denote beg of round.
Work (k2, p2) rib for 10 rounds.
Beg working in st st (k every round with RS facing throughout), until work measures approx. 17in (43cm).
Work (k2, p2) rib for 10 rounds.
Bind (cast) off in rib.

FINISHING

Block and sew in any yarn ends.

cable bag

I love chunky cable knit bags, especially when they have bright pink girly pompoms on the front!

FOR THE BAG

(make 2, front and back)
Cast on 33 sts.
Knit in garter st (every row k) for 5 rows.
Inc row (WS): Kfb in each of first 2 sts, k1, [kfb in next st, k1] 6 times, kfb in each of next 3 sts, k1, [kfb in next st, k1] 6 times, kfb in each of next 2 sts. *52 sts.*

START CABLE PATT
Row 1 (RS): P2, *k9, p4; rep from * ending last rep with p2.
Row 2 (WS): K2, *p9, k4; rep from * ending last rep with k2.
Row 3: P2, *yo, C6B, k3, p4; rep from * ending last rep with p2.
Row 4: Rep Row 2.
Row 5: Rep Row 1.
Row 6: Rep Row 2.
Row 7: P2, *k3, C6F, p4; rep from * ending last rep with p2.
Row 8: Rep Row 2.
Rep Rows 1–8 until work measures approx. 12in (30.5cm), ending on a Row 1.
Dec row (RS): [K2tog] twice, [k1, k2tog] 6 times, [k2tog] 3 times, [k1, k2tog] 6 times, k2, [k2tog] twice. *33 sts.*
Knit in garter st for 5 rows.
Bind (cast) off.

FOR THE HANDLES

(make two)
Using A, cast on 6 sts.
Work in st st until handle measures 31in (79cm).
Bind (cast) off.

FINISHING

Add a fabric lining to the knitted bag and the handles, as described on page 125.

Make 3 small pompoms using a pompom maker. Sew onto the garter stitch section, one in the middle at the top of the bag and one at each end above the first and last cable.

SKILL RATING ● ● ●

MATERIALS

Caron Chunky Cakes (100% acrylic, approx. 296yds/271m per 9⅞oz/280g ball) bulky (chunky) weight yarn
 1 ball of 17004 Lime Cream

Scraps of pink yarn to make pompoms

US size 11 (8mm) knitting needles

Yarn sewing needle

Lining fabric for main piece and handles

Sewing needle and thread to match fabric

2½in (6cm) diameter pompom maker

FINISHED MEASUREMENTS

Approx. 13in (33cm) wide x 14in (35.5cm) deep

GAUGE (TENSION)

10 sts x 16 rows over a 4in (10cm) square in garter stitch, using US size 11 (8mm) needles.

ABBREVIATIONS

approx.	approximately
dec	decrease
inc	increase
k	knit
k2tog	knit 2 stitches together
kfb	knit into front and back of next stitch
p	purl
patt	pattern
rep	repeat
RS	right side
sl	slip
st(s)	stitch(es)
st st	stockinette (stocking) stitch
WS	wrong side
yo	yarn over
[ ]	repeat sequence between square brackets the number of times stated

SPECIAL ABBREVIATIONS

C6B: cable 6 back: sl next 3 sts purlwise onto cable needle and hold in back, k3, k3 from cable needle
C6F: cable 6 front: sl next 3 sts purlwise onto cable needle and hold in front, k3, k3 from cable needle

chunky gloves

I love these gloves; they're just the right sort of chunkiness. Follow the first number each time to knit the smaller size for a woman, or follow the second number in bold to make a larger size for a man. If there's just one number, it's for both sizes.

SKILL RATING ● ● ●

MATERIALS

Schoppel Wolle Reggae Ombre (100% merino wool, approx. 109yds/100m per 1¾oz/50g ball) aran (worsted) weight yarn
  2 balls of 1701 Parrot

Set of 4 US size 4 (3.5mm) and US size 6 (4mm) double-pointed needles

Stitch holder

Yarn sewing needle

FINISHED MEASUREMENTS

To fit size: S (woman):**L (man)**

GAUGE (TENSION)

20 sts x 32 rows over a 4in (10cm) square in stockinette (stocking) stitch, using US size 6 (4mm) needles.

ABBREVIATIONS

beg	beginning
dec	decrease
k	knit
k2tog	knit 2 stitches together
M1	make a stitch
p	purl
patt	pattern
prev	prev
rem	remain
rep	repeat
RS	right side
sl	slip
sl2 k1 p2sso	slip 2 stitches, knit 1 st, pass 2 slipped stitches over
SM	slip marker
st(s)	stitch(es)
st st	stockinette (stocking) stitch
WS	wrong side
[ ]	rep sequence between square brackets the number of times stated

FOR THE LEFT GLOVE

Using US size 4 (3.5mm) double-pointed needles, cast on 14:**16** sts on each of first two needles and 16:**20** sts on third needle. Join round, place marker to denote beg of round. *44:**52** sts.*
Work 19:**22** rounds in [k2, p2] rib.

CHANGE TO ST ST (every round k)
K 5:**7** rounds.
Change to US size 6 (4mm) needles.
K 3:**5** rounds.**
Next round: K21:**25**, place marker, M1, place marker, k23:**27**. *45:**53** sts.*
***Next round:** K to end.
Next round: K to marker, SM, M1, k to marker, M1, SM, k to end. *47:**55** sts.*
Rep last 2 rounds until 53:**63** sts rem.
Next round: K to end.
Next round: K to marker, remove marker, sl next 9:**11** sts of thumb gusset onto st holder, remover marker, cast on 1:**2** sts, k to end. *45:**54** sts.*
Arrange sts evenly across 3 needles.
K 3:**4** rounds.
Change to US size 4 (3.5mm) double-pointed needles.
K 3:**4** rounds.***

DIVIDE FOR FINGERS

Little finger: Using first needle k5:**6**, cast on 3 sts and put on second needle, leave next 36:**43** sts of round on st holder; using next needle: k last 4:**5** sts. *12:**14** sts.*
K 18:**20** rounds.
Dec round: [K2tog] 0:**1** time, [sl2 k1 p2sso] 4 times. *4:**5** sts.*
Cut yarn leaving a long end, thread end through rem sts, draw up and secure.

tips

Leave the other stitches on holders and complete the thumb and fingers individually.

When working in the round the RS is always facing, so to get the look of stockinette (stocking) stitch you'll need to knit every round.

Ring finger: With little finger on right and RS facing, using first needle, k first 5:**6** sts from st holder, leaving next 26:**31** sts on holder, cast on 3 sts; using second needle, k3 from spare needle; using third needle k2:**3** from spare needle, k up 4 sts from base of 3 sts cast on for prev finger, sl 3 cast-on sts onto second needle. *17:**19** sts.*
Next round: K to end.
Next round: K5:**6**, sl2 k1 p2sso, k6:**7**, sl2 k1 p2sso. *13:**15** sts.*
K 22:**24** rounds.
Dec round: K1:0, [sl2 k1 p2sso] 4:**5** times. *5:**5** sts.*
Fasten off as little finger.

Middle finger: With little finger on right, with RS facing, using first needle, k first 6:**7** sts from st holder, leaving center 14:**16** sts on holder, cast on 3 sts; using second needle, k3 from spare needle; using third needle, k3:**5** from spare needle, k up 4 sts from base of 3 sts cast on for prev finger, sl 3 cast-on stitches onto second needle. *19:**22** sts.*
K 24:**26** rounds.
Dec round: K1, [sl2 k1 p2sso] 6:**7** times. *7:**8** sts.*
Fasten off as prev finger.

Forefinger: With little finger on right and RS facing, using first needle, k first 6:**7** sts from spare needle; using second needle, k6:**7** from spare needle; using third needle k2:**2** from spare needle, pick up and k 3:**4** sts from base of 3 sts cast on for prev finger. *17:**20** sts.*
Next round: K to end.
Next round: K14:**17**, sl2 k1 p2sso. *15:**18** sts.*
K 22:**24** rounds.
Dec round: [Sl2 k1 p2sso] 5:**6** times. *5:**6** sts.*
Fasten off as little finger.

Thumb: With fingers on left, using first needle, k6:**6** from thumb st holder; using second needle, k3:**5** from spare needle, pick up and k 3 sts from row ends; using third needle, pick up and k 2 sts from cast on and 3 sts from front row ends. *17:**19** sts.*
K 16:**18** rounds.
Dec round: [Sl2 k1 p2sso] 5:**6** times, k2tog:**k1**. *6:**7** sts.*
Fasten off as little finger.

FOR THE RIGHT GLOVE

Work as given for left glove to **.
Next round: K23:**27**, place marker, M1, place marker, k21:**25**. *45:**53** sts.*
Work as left glove from *** to ***.
Divide for fingers:
Little finger: Using first needle, k4:**5**, cast on 3 sts and put on second needle, leave next 36:**43** sts of round on st holder, using next needle, k last 5:**6** sts. *12:**14** sts.*
Complete fingers and thumbs as for left glove.

FINISHING

Block and sew in any yarn ends.

lace scarf

This scarf drapes really nicely and it's light, which makes it very comfortable to wear. It's nice and wide too, so can double up as a shawl in the summer months. The lace border is knitted separately and sewn on.

SKILL RATING ● ● ●

MATERIALS

Scheepjes Whirl (60% cotton, 40% acrylic, approx. 1093yds/1000m per 7¾oz/220g ball) fingering (4 ply) weight yarn
  1 ball of 752 Raspberry Rocky Road

US size 6 (4mm) knitting needles

Yarn sewing needle

FINISHED MEASUREMENTS

Approx. 20¾in (53cm) wide

GAUGE (TENSION)

22 sts x 30 rows over a 4in (10cm) square in pattern, using US size 6 (4mm) needles.

ABBREVIATIONS

approx.	approximately
k	knit
k2tog	knit 2 stitches together
p	purl
rep	repeat
RS	right side
sl1	slip 1 stitch
sl2 k1 p2sso	slip 2 stitches, knit 1 stitch, pass 2 slipped stitches over
ssk	slip slip knit
st(s)	stitch(es)
WS	wrong side
yo	yarn over
yf	yarn forward
[ ]	repeat sequence between square brackets the number of times stated

FOR THE SCARF

Cast on 117 sts loosely.

K 4 rows.

Row 1 and every other WS row: K3, p to last 3 sts, k3.

Row 2: K3, [k5, yo, ssk, k3] 11 times, k4.

Row 3: Rep Row 1.

Row 4: K3, [k3, k2tog, yo, k1, yo, ssk, k2] 11 times, k4.

Row 5: Rep Row 1.

Row 6: K3, [k2, k2tog, yo, k3, yo, ssk, k1] 11 times, k4.

Row 7: Rep Row 1.

Row 8: K3, [k1, k2tog, yo, k5, yo, ssk] 11 times, k4.

Row 9: Rep Row 1.

Row 10 (RS): K3, k2tog, yo, k7 [yo, sl2 k1 p2sso, yo, k7] 10 times, yo, ssk, k3.

Rep Rows 1–10 until scarf measures approx. 57½in (146cm), ending on a Row 1 (WS).

K 4 rows.

Bind (cast) off.

FOR THE EDGING

(make 2)

Cast on 10 sts.

NB: Stitches should only be counted after the 8th row.

Row 1 (RS): Sl1, k2, yo, k2tog, *(yf, wrap yarn around right needle once more), k2tog; rep from * once more, k1.

Row 2: K3, [p1, k2] twice, yo, k2tog, k1.

Row 3: Sl1, k2, yo, k2tog, k2, *(yf, wrap yarn around right needle once more), k2tog; rep from * once more, k1.

Row 4: K3, p1, k2, p1, k4, yo, k2tog, k1.

Row 5: Sl1, k2, yo, k2tog, k4, *(yf, wrap yarn around right needle once more), k2tog; rep from * once more, k1.

Row 6: K3, p1, k2, p1, k6, yo, k2tog, k1.

Row 7: Sl1, k2, yo, k2tog, k11.

Row 8: Bind (cast) off 6 sts, k6, (not including st on needle after binding/casting off), yo, k2tog, k1. *10 sts.*

Rep these 8 rows 14 more times, or until edging matches width of main piece.

Bind (cast) off.

FINISHING

Pin and block the edging.

Place one short edge of the main piece with RS facing upward on a flat surface. Lay one edging piece with RS facing upward on top of the main piece, overlapping one row of the main piece. Pin the edging along the edge and sew together using a running stitch. Add the second edge in the same way.

Gently press the joins and scarf edges.

MATERIALS

Schoppel Wolle Reggae Ombre (100% merino wool, approx. 109yds/100m per 1¾oz/50g ball) worsted (aran) weight yarn
  2 balls of 2357 Rays of Light

Set of 4 US size 8 (5mm) double-pointed needles

Yarn sewing needle

FINISHED MEASUREMENTS

Approx. 14in (36cm) long

GAUGE (TENSION)

24 sts x 32 rows over a 4in (10cm) square in stockinette (stocking) stitch, using US size 8 (5mm) needles.

ABBREVIATIONS

approx.	approximately
k	knit
st(s)	stitch(es)
st st	stockinette (stocking) stitch

arm warmers

These are an absolute "must-have" for those in colder climates in the middle of winter. They are bright and cheerful, and functional, too!

FOR THE ARM WARMERS

(make 2)
Cast on 36 sts divided equally over 3 needles. Join round, taking care not to twist sts.
Work in st st (every round k) until work measures approx. 14in (36cm).
Bind (cast) off.

FINISHING

Block and sew in any yarn ends.

pompom scarf

This is a lovely stitch that looks good on either side—so there is no obvious wrong or right way round to wear it, which is ideal for a scarf.

SKILL RATING ● ● ●

MATERIALS

Bernat Softee Baby Stripes (100% acrylic, approx. 286yds/262m per 4¼oz/120g ball) DK (light worsted) weight yarn
  2 balls of 53016 Blue Jeans Stripe

US size 6 (4mm) knitting needles

Yarn sewing needle

Approx. 17in (43cm) bobble trim

FINISHED MEASUREMENTS

Approx. 8in (20cm) wide x 72in (182cm) long

GAUGE (TENSION)

23 sts x 25 rows over a 4in (10cm) square in patt, using US size 6 (4mm) needles.

ABBREVIATIONS

approx.	approximately
k	knit
p	purl
patt	pattern
rep	repeat
RS	right side
sl2p	slip 2 stitches, purlwise with yarn in back
st(s)	stitch(es)
WS	wrong side

FOR THE SCARF

Cast on 46 sts.

K 1 row.

Row 1 (RS): K2, *p2, k2; rep from * to end.

Row 2 (WS): K2, *k2, sl2p (keeping yarn at back); rep from * to last 4 sts, k4.

Rows 1 and 2 form patt, rep them until work measures approx. 72in (182cm), finishing on a Row 2.

K 1 row.

Bind (cast) off.

FINISHING

Block and sew in any yarn ends.

Sew bobble trim to each end of scarf.

chapter 2
for the home

herringbone pillow cover

This is a really thick, padded stitch that makes a great pillow cover. The bright pink pompom edging zings out against the lovely greens; a tassel edging would work equally well. I've backed my pillow with fabric, but you could make a second panel for the back instead— although you'll then need twice as much yarn.

FOR THE COVER

Knit very loosely throughout.
Cast on 62 sts.
Row 1: Sl first st knitwise, sl next st knitwise, insert LH needle, from left to right, into front of both slipped sts and k2tog but drop only one loop off needle, *sl next st purlwise, sl next st knitwise, insert LH needle, from left to right, into front of both slipped sts and k2tog, but drop only one loop off needle; rep from * to last st, k into back of last st.
Row 2: *P2tog but drop only first loop off needle; rep from * to last st, p last st.
Rep Rows 1 and 2 until work measures 16in (40cm).
Bind (cast) off.

FINISHING

Use the knitted piece as a template to cut the lining fabric, allowing an extra ⅝in (1.5cm) seam allowance on each side. Pin and then hand-sew the pompom edging all around on the RS edge of the fabric, with the pompoms facing inward and working within the seam allowance.

With RS together, pin the knitted piece and the fabric pieces together, making sure the pompoms are on the RS between the layers. Sew around three sides with a ⅝in (1.5cm) seam allowance.

Turn RS out and insert the pillow form. Sew the last side together neatly, enclosing the pillow form.

SKILL RATING ● ● ●

MATERIALS

Caron Chunky Cakes (100% acrylic, approx. 296yds/271m per 9⅞oz/280g ball) bulky (chunky) weight yarn
  1 ball of 17004 Lime Cream

US size 11 (8mm) knitting needles

Yarn sewing needle

Approx. 17in (45cm) square of lining fabric

Approx. 70in (180cm) of bright pink pompom edging

16in (40cm) square pillow form

FINISHED MEASUREMENT

To fit 16in (40cm) square pillow form

GAUGE (TENSION)

15 sts x 12 rows over a 4in (10cm) square in herringbone stitch, using US size 11 (8mm) needles.

ABBREVIATIONS

approx.	approximately
k	knit
k2tog	knit 2 stitches together
LH	left hand
p	purl
p2tog	purl 2 stitches together
rep	repeat
RS	right side
sl	slip
st(s)	stitch(es)

MATERIALS

Bernat Softee Baby Stripes (100% acrylic, approx. 286yds/262m per 4¼oz/120g ball) light worsted (DK) weight yarn
  1 ball of 53007 Sunny Side Up

US size 4 (3.5mm) knitting needles

Set of 4 US size 4 (3.5mm) double-pointed needles

Yarn sewing needle

Child's wooden coat hanger, 12in (30.5cm) long

Approx. 26 x 14in (65 x 35cm) lining fabric

FINISHED MEASUREMENTS

Approx. 12 x 12in (30.5 x 30.5cm)

GAUGE (TENSION)

Each square measures approx. 3in (7cm) square, using US size 4 (3.5mm) needles.

ABBREVIATIONS

alt	alternate
approx.	approximately
cont	continue
k	knit
rep	repeat
RS	right side
sl1p	slip 1 st purlwise with yarn in front
sl2togkpo	with yarn at back, slip 2 sts tog knitwise, knit 1 stitch, pass 2 slipped stitches over
st(s)	stitch(es)
tbl	through back of loop

peg bag

This bright peg bag is perfect for summer washing lines. If you knit from the inside strand and outside strands of the balls of yarn, it adds more color variety.

FOR THE SQUARE

(make 32)
Using US size 4 (3.5mm) straight knitting needles, cast on 31 sts.
Row 1: K to end.
Row 2: Sl1p, k13, sl2togkpo, k13, k1 tbl. *29 sts.*
Row 3 and all alt rows: Sl1p, k to last st, k1tbl.
Row 4: Sl1p, k12, sl2togkpo, k12, k1tbl. *27 sts.*
Row 6: Sl1p, k11, sl2togkpo, k11, k1tbl. *25 sts.*
Row 8: Sl1p, k10, sl2togkpo, k10, k1tbl. *23 sts.*
Row 9: Sl1p, k to last st, k1tbl.

tip

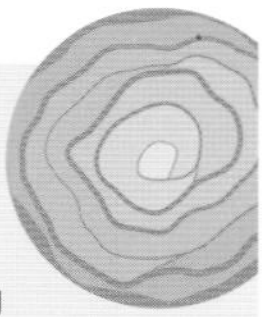

These squares can be knitted in one color; if you prefer a two-color square, cut the yarn at the color break of your choice and join as per the instructions above. If making lots of two-color squares you may need two balls of yarn.

tip
The back and front panels are the
same, except the front panel has an
opening for the pegs.

To change color here, cut yarn and join another strand in a different colorway further along ball.

Row 10: Sl1p, k9, sl2togkpo, k9, k1tbl. *21 sts.*
Row 11: Cont to rep Row 3 on every foll alt row.
Row 12: Sl1p, k8, sl2togkpo, k8, k1tbl. *19 sts.*
Row 14: Sl1p, k7, sl2togkpo, k7, k1tbl. *17 sts.*
Row 16: Sl1p, k6, sl2togkpo, k6, k1tbl. *15 sts.*
Row 18: Sl1p, k5, sl2togkpo, k5, k1tbl. *13 sts.*
Row 20: Sl1p, k4, sl2togkpo, k4, k1tbl. *11 sts.*
Row 22: Sl1p, k3, sl2togkpo, k3, k1tbl. *9 sts.*
Row 24: Sl1p, k2, sl2togkpo, k2, k1tbl. *7 sts.*
Row 26: Sl1p, k1, sl2togkpo, k1, k1tbl. *5 sts.*
Row 28: Sl1p, sl2togkpo, k1tbl. *3 sts.*
Row 30: Sl2togkpo.
Cut yarn and pull through last st to fasten off.

FINISHING

For the back, lay out four squares across by four squares down. With RS together and a yarn sewing needle and matching yarn, join the squares in horizontal rows and then in vertical rows.

For the front, join the squares as for back, but leave top centre two squares open across the bottom to form a horizontal opening for the pegs. Using US size 4 (3.5mm) double-pointed needles, with the RS of the front facing and working around the opening, pick up 20 sts each on the first and second needles and 23 sts on the third needle.

Sl last st over the first st made to join the round, place marker to denote beg of round. *62 sts.*
P 1 round.
Bind (cast) off.

With RS together, using a yarn sewing needle and matching yarn, sew the bottom edge only of the back and front together.

ADD THE LINING
Use the knitted piece to cut the lining, allowing ⅞in (2cm) extra all round for seams. Sew the lining onto the knitted piece. Cut a slit in the lining to match the pocket opening in the knitting. Fold the lining edge to the WS around the opening and pin, then neatly sew it down around the opening.

With RS together, fold the piece along the bottom seam and join the side and top seams, leaving an opening at the center of the top for the coat hanger hook. Insert the hanger through the pocket opening, taking the hook through the hole at the top to the right side.

tip
When sewing the lining onto the main piece, make sure you allow enough room for the coat hanger.

bobble blanket

These rich fall colors work really well for a cozy blanket and the colors from this brand of yarn throw up some interesting shades of bobble.

FOR THE BLANKET

Using US size 8 (5mm) straight needles, cast on 209 sts.
Work 4 rows of st st, starting with RS k row and ending with WS p row.
*Bobble row A: K5, [MB, k5] to end of row. *34 bobbles.*
Work 11 rows of st st, starting and ending with p row.
Bobble Row B: K8, [MB, k5] to last 8 sts, k last 8 sts. *33 bobbles.*
Work 11 rows of st st, starting and ending with p row.
Rep from * until total of 261 rows, or until blanket measures approx. 44in (112cm), ending on a k row. Work last k row on circular needle ready to start working in round.
Place marker in last st to denote first corner.
Do not bind (cast) off.

SKILL RATING ● ● ●

MATERIALS

Schoppel Wolle Reggae Ombre (100% merino wool, approx. 109yds/100m per 1¾oz/50g ball) worsted (aran) weight yarn
  20 balls of 1701 Parrot

US size 8 (5mm) straight knitting needles

3 x US size 8 (5mm) circular knitting needles, 40in (100cm) long

4 stitch markers

Yarn sewing needle

FINISHED MEASUREMENTS

Approx. 51 x 48in (130 x 122cm) including 2in (5cm) border around

GAUGE (TENSION)

17 sts x 24 rows over a 4in (10cm) square in pattern, using US size 8 (5mm) needles.

ABBREVIATIONS

approx.	approximately
beg	beginning
k	knit
k2tog	knit 2 stitches together
kfb	knit into front and back of next stitch
p	purl
p2tog	purl 2 stitches together
rep	repeat
RS	right side
st(s)	stitch(es)
st st	stockinette (stocking) stitch
tbl	through back of loop
WS	wrong side
yo	yarn over
[ ]	repeat sequence between square brackets the number of times stated

SPECIAL ABBREVIATION

MB: make bobble: *[Yo, k1] 3 times in same st; turn work so WS is facing you, slip 1 purlwise, p5; turn work so RS is facing you, slip 1 purlwise, k5; turn work so WS is facing you, [p2tog] 3 times; turn work so RS is facing you, slip 1 purlwise, k2tog, pass slipped stitch over

ADD BORDER

Use 3 circular needles around border; 2 needles to hold sts and one working needle.

Continuing with first circular needle, pick up 195 sts along side edge (3 for every 4 rows), place marker to denote 2nd corner.

Using second circular needle, pick up 209 sts along bottom edge, place marker to denote 3rd corner.

Pick up 195 sts up side place marker to denote 4th corner and beg of round. *808 sts.*

Starting with p row, k for 17 rows, kfb in st on each side of marker and ending on a p row.

Loosely bind (cast) off all sts as foll: *k2tog tbl, place st back on left needle, rep from * to end of round.

On last st, cut yarn and pull end through, then sew into opposite st.

FINISHING

Block and sew in any yarn ends.

bobble laptop cozy

I love knitted laptop cozies; I have absolutely no idea why people would want
a leather cover for their laptop when you can have a knitted one like this!
Bobble stitch is perfect to give your laptop the absolutely best protection.

MATERIALS

Caron Chunky Cakes (100% acrylic, approx. 296yds/271m per 9⅞oz/280g ball) bulky (chunky) weight yarn
  1 ball of 17009 Sweet & Sour

US size 11 (8mm) knitting needles

Yarn sewing needle

16 x 20in (40 x 50.5cm) of cotton lining fabric

Approx. 1yd (1m) of bright pink ribbon

FINISHED MEASUREMENTS

Approx. 13 x 9in (33 x 23cm)

To fit an 11in (27.5cm) MacBook Air

GAUGE (TENSION)

12 sts x 18 rows over a 4in (10cm) square in pattern, using US size 11 (8mm) needles.

ABBREVIATIONS

approx.	approximately
k	knit
LH	left hand
p	purl
rep	repeat
RH	right hand
RS	right side
st(s)	stitch(es)
yo	yarn over

SPECIAL ABBREVIATION

MB: make bobble: start to k next st, but do not slip loop off needle, yo (to front), insert needle in st again knitwise, yo and k st, but do not slip loop off needle, yo (to front), insert needle in st again knitwise, yo and k st, slip st off needle to finish st (5 sts). Turn work, yo (to back), knit these 5 sts. Turn work, yo (to back), knit next 2 sts tog, slip knitted st from RH needle onto LH needle, slip each of next 3 sts over k st separately, k this st to complete bobble

FOR THE COVER

Cast on 37 sts.
Row 1: K to end.
Row 2: P to end.
Row 3: K2, MB in next st, *k3, MB in next st: rep from * to last 2 sts, k2.
Row 4: P to end.
Row 5: K4, MB in next st, *k3, MB in next st; rep from * to last 4 sts, k4.
Row 6: P to end.
Rep Rows 3–6 until 33 bobble rows have been worked, or work measures approx. 26in (66cm).
Next row: P to end.
Bind (cast) off.

FINISHING

Sew in all ends.

With RS together, fold the knitted piece in half so that the cast on and bound (cast) off edges meet, then sew the side seams. Turn RS out.

ADD THE LINING

Make up the fabric lining as described on page 125. Insert the lining into the knitted piece with WS together. Cut the ribbon in half, or to the desired length. Insert one end of the ribbon at the center top between the lining and the knitted piece on each side and pin in place. Hand stitch the lining and knitted piece together along the top edge, securing the ribbon at the same time. Trim the ends of the ribbon into a V to stop it fraying.

Add two or three hand stitches in sewing thread on each side of the bottom edges to secure the lining to the knitted piece and keep it in position.

MATERIALS

Caron Big Cakes (100% acrylic, approx. 603yds/551m per 10½oz/300g ball) worsted (aran) weight yarn
   3 balls of 26003 Honey Glazed

US size 8 (5mm) circular knitting needle, 60in (150cm) long

Yarn sewing needle

FINISHED MEASUREMENTS

Approx. 44 x 47in (112 x 120cm)

GAUGE (TENSION)

22 sts x 18 rows over a 4in (10cm) square in chevron pattern, using US size 8 (5mm) needles.

ABBREVIATIONS

approx.	approximately
k	knit
k2tog	knit 2 stitches together
p	purl
rep	repeat
st(s)	stitch(es)
yo	yarn over
[ ]	repeat sequence between square brackets the number of times stated

NOTE

To make the blanket larger or smaller, the multiple for this stitch is 18 sts plus 2.

chevron blanket

This blanket is so cozy, with beautiful colors and in a really easy stitch to work. I want to make loads of these!

FOR THE BLANKET

Cast on 236 sts.
Row 1 (RS): K.
Row 2: K1, p to last st, k1.
Row 3: K1, *[k2tog] 3 times, [yo, k1] 6 times, [k2tog] 3 times; rep from * to last st, k1.
Row 4: K.
Rows 5–8: Rep Rows 1–4.
Rep Rows 1–8 until blanket measures approx. 47in (120cm), finishing on a Row 8.
Bind (cast) off.

FINISHING

Block and sew in any yarn ends.

hot water bottle cover

It's important to have a really thick and cozy stitch to protect cold toes from direct heat. I've made one side of this cover in a lovely thick lattice stitch and on the other side I've worked a simple rib. Both show the changing yarn colors really well.

FOR THE RIBBING SIDE

Using US size 8 (5mm) needles, cast on 38 sts,
Work in (k1, p1) rib until work measures approx. 13½in (34cm) or length of hot water bottle.
Bind (cast) off using US size 6 (4mm) needles.

FOR THE CLOSE-WOVEN BASKET LATTICE SIDE

Using US size 8 (5mm) needles, cast on 50 sts.
Row 1 (WS): K2, *p4, k2; rep from * to end.
Row 2: P2, *C4B; p2; rep from * to end.
Row 3 and all foll WS rows: K knit sts and p purl sts.
Row 4: P1, *BC, FC; rep from * ending, p1.
Row 5: Rep Row 3.
Row 6: P1, k2, p2, *C4F, p2; rep from *, ending k2, p1.
Row 7: Rep Row 3.
Row 8: P1, *FC, BC; rep from * to end, p1.
Rep Rows 1–8 until work measures approx. 13½in (34cm) or to length of hot water bottle.
Bind (cast) off using US size 6 (4mm) needles.

FINISHING

Block and sew in any yarn ends.

With RS together, sew the cover together around the sides and bottom. Turn RS out and insert the hot water bottle.

Thread the ribbon through a suitable hole in the knitting on both sides at the neck of the cover. Gather and tie into a bow at the front.

SKILL RATING ● ● ●

MATERIALS

Caron Cakes (100% acrylic, approx. 382yds/350m per 7oz/200g ball) worsted (aran) weight yarn
  1 ball of 17024 Mixed Berry

US size 6 (4mm) and US size 8 (5mm) knitting needles

Cable needle

Yarn sewing needle

1yd (1m) of velvet ribbon

FINISHED MEASUREMENTS

13½ x 9in (34 x 23cm)

To fit a 4 pint (1.8 liter) hot water bottle

GAUGE (TENSION)

18 sts x 22 rows over a 4in (10cm) square in ribbing (stretched flat), using US size 8 (5mm) needles.

ABBREVIATIONS

approx.	approximately
cont	continue
k	knit
p	purl
rem	remain
rep	repeat
RS	right side
sl	slip
st(s)	stitch(es)

SPECIAL ABBREVIATIONS

C4B: cable 4 back: sl next 2 sts onto cable needle, and hold to back, k2, k2 from cable needle
C4F: cable 4 front: sl next 2 sts onto cable needle, and hold in front, k2, k2 from cable needle
BC: back cross: sl 1 st onto cable needle and hold to back, k2, then p st from cable needle
FC: front cross: sl next 2 sts onto cable needle and hold in front, p1, k2 from cable needle

pebbles pillow cover

A lovely, big, chunky pillow cover, which is knitted from corner to corner using subtle neutral tones.

MATERIALS

Bernat Blanket Stripes (100% polyester, approx. 220yds/201m per 10½oz/300g ball) super bulky (super chunky) weight yarn
  2 balls of 76023 Buffed Stone

US size 11 (8mm) knitting needles

Yarn sewing needle

20in (50.5cm) pillow form

FINISHED MEASUREMENTS

To fit size 20in (50.5cm) pillow form

GAUGE (TENSION)

8 sts x 16 rows over a 4in (10cm) square in garter stitch, using US size 11 (8mm) needles.

ABBREVIATIONS

approx.	approximately
beg	beginning
dec	decrease
inc	increase
k	knit
k2tog	knit 2 stitches together
kfb	knit into the front and back of the next stitch
rem	remain
rep	repeat
RS	right side
st(s)	stitch(es)

FOR THE PILLOW COVER

(make 2, front and back)
Cast on 2 sts.
Row 1 (inc): Kfb in first st, k to end.
Rep Row 1 until sides measure 20in (50.5cm).
Next row (dec): K2tog, k to end.
Rep this row until 2 sts rem.
Next row: K2tog.
Bind (cast) off.

FINISHING

Block and sew in any yarn ends.

Place the two pieces RS together and sew around three sides. Turn RS out and insert the pillow form. Sew the remaining side.

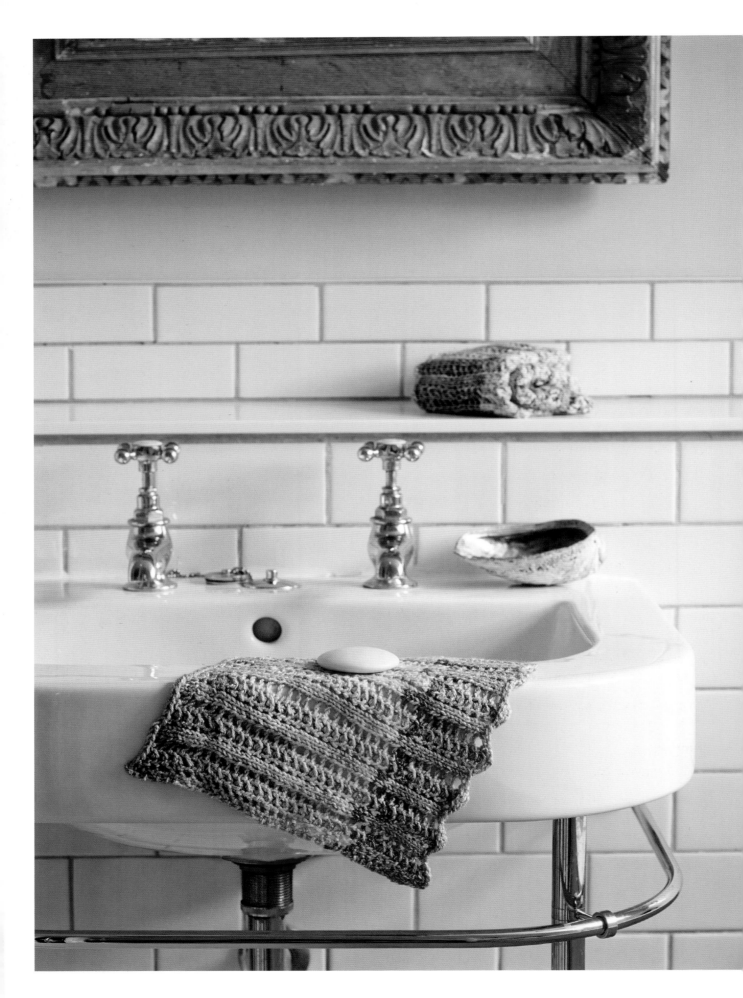

ecological washcloths

It's very hard to find recycleable cloths in the supermarket, so why not just make your own! So simple—and they make amazing gifts, too.

FOR THE WASHCLOTH

Using US size 6 (4mm) needles, cast on 51 sts.
Row 1: K.
Row 2: P1, k to last st, p1.
Row 3: P1, k1, *k2, yo, p1, p3tog, p1,yo; rep from * to last 2 sts, k1, p1.
Row 4: P1, k to last st, p1.
Rep Rows 3 and 4 until work measures 8in (20cm), finishing on an even row.
Bind (cast) off loosely, otherwise it will pull the fabric in when blocked to width.

FINISHING

Sew in any yarn ends.

Block to a square, but do not use steam with this yarn.

SKILL RATING ● ● ○

MATERIALS
James C Brett Harmony DK (78% acrylic, 22% cotton, approx. 284yds/260m per 3½oz/100g ball) light worsted (DK) weight yarn
  1 ball of HY5

US size 6 (4mm) knitting needles

Yarn sewing needle

GAUGE (TENSION)
25 sts x 27 rows over a 4in (10cm) square in pattern, using US size 6 (4mm) needles.

FINISHED MEASUREMENTS
8 x 8in (20 x 20cm)

ABBREVIATIONS

approx.	approximately
k	knit
p	purl
p3tog	purl 3 stitches together
rep	repeat
st(s)	stitch(es)
yo	yarn over

garter stitch blanket

This blanket is made by knitting up big rectangles and sewing them together, which gives a really interesting mix of colors. It's a really simple blanket to make—and if you don't like having a big heavy piece on your lap while you're knitting, or if you're knitting in the middle of the summer, this is the ideal blanket project for you.

MATERIALS

Caron Big Cakes (100% acrylic, approx. 603yds/551m per 10½oz/ 300g ball) worsted (aran) weight yarn
   5 balls of 26018 Summer Berry Tart

US size 8 (5mm) knitting needles

Yarn sewing needle

FINISHED MEASUREMENTS

Approx. 51½ x 64in (131 x 164cm)

Each rectangle measures approx. 16 x 25¾in (41 x 65.5cm)

GAUGE (TENSION)

16 sts x 32 rows over a 4in (10cm) square in garter stitch, using US size 8 (5mm) needles.

ABBREVIATIONS

approx.	approximately
k	knit
p	purl
RS	right side
st(s)	stitch(es)

FOR THE RECTANGLES

(make 8)
Cast on 105 sts.
Work in garter st (every row k) until work measures 16in (41cm).
Bind (cast) off.

FINISHING

Block and sew in any yarn ends.

Lay out the rectangles two wide by four long. With RS together, join the horizontal seams, and then join the central vertical seam.

to wear

lace cardigan

This is a fine and delicate cardigan in rich colors. It is worked in a pretty and subtle lace stitch that complements the color changes.

SKILL RATING ● ● ●

MATERIALS

Schoppel Wolle Zauberball 100 (100% wool, approx. 437yds/400m per 3½oz/100g ball) light fingering (3-ply) weight yarn
  3 balls of 2309 Blue Lagoon

US size 2/3 (3mm) and US size 2 (2.75mm) knitting needles

Stitch holder

Yarn sewing needle

4 buttons

FINISHED MEASUREMENTS

To fit						
US size:	6	**8**	10	**12**	14	**16**
UK size:	8	**10**	12	**14**	16	**18**
ACTUAL MEASUREMENTS						
Bust:	33¾	**36¼**	38¼	**40¼**	42	**44in**
	86	**92**	97	**102**	107	**112cm**
Length to	19	**19¼**	19¼	**20**	20	**20¾in**
shoulder:	48	**49**	49	**51**	51	**53cm**
Sleeve length:	17¼	**17¾**	18	**18**	18½	**19in**
	44	**45**	46	**46**	47	**48cm**

GAUGE (TENSION)

28 sts x 36 rows over a 4in (10cm) square in stockinette (stocking) stitch, using US size 2/3 (3mm) needles.

ABBREVIATIONS

beg	beginning	**sl1 k1 psso**	slip 1 stitch, knit 1 st, pass slipped stitch over
cont	continue		
dec	decrease	**ssk**	slip 1 kwise, slip 1 kwise, k2tog through back of loop
foll	follow(s)ing		
inc	increase		
k	knit	**st(s)**	stitch(es)
k2tog	knit 2 stitches together	**st st**	stocking (stockinette) stitch
M1	make one st		
p	purl	**WS**	wrong side
patt	pattern	**yo**	yarn over
rem	remain(ing)	**[ ]**	repeat sequence between square brackets the number of times stated
rep	repeat		
RH	right hand		

FOR THE CARDIGAN

Using US size 2/3 (3mm) needles, cast on 220(**238**:247:**256**:274:**283**) sts.
Row 1: [K1, p1] seed (moss) st to last 0(**0**:1:**0**:0:**1**) st, k0(**0**:1:**0**:0:**1**).
Row 2: K0(**0**:1:**0**:0:**1**), [p1, k1] to end.
Rep Rows 1 and 2 once more.

START LACE PATT

Row 1: K3, *yo, k2, sl1 k1 psso, k2tog, k2, yo, k1; rep from * to last st, k1.
Row 2 (WS): P.

Row 3: K2, *yo, k2, sl1 k1 psso, k2tog, k2, yo, k1; rep from * to last 2 sts, k2.
Row 4: P.
Cont in lace patt as set by these 4 rows until work measures 11½(**11½**:11¼:**12**:11½:**12**)in/29.5(**29.5**:28.5:**30.5**:29.5:**30.5**)cm, ending with Row 4 of patt.
Cont in st st starting with a k row.
Next row: K1(**2**:2:**127**:1:**1**), k2tog, *k52(**31**:58:**–**:43:**137**), k2tog, rep from * 4(**7**:4:**–**:6:**2**) times, k to end.
*215(**230**:242:**255**:267:**280**) sts.*
P one row.
Split for front and back working in st st as foll:

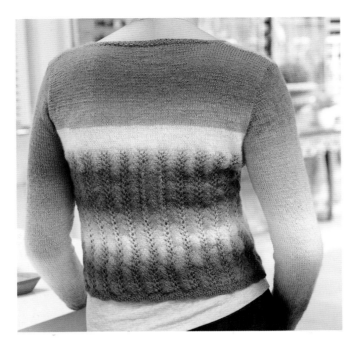

RIGHT FRONT

Next row: K53(**57**:60:**63**:66:**69**), turn and work on these sts only, leaving rem on holder or spare needle.

ARMHOLE SHAPING

Next row (WS): Bind (cast) off 4(**4**:5:**5**:6:**7**) sts, p to end. *49(**53**:55:**58**:60:**62**) sts.*

Next row: K to last 2 sts, k2tog. *48(**52**:54:**57**:59:**61**) sts.*

Next row: P.

Cont to dec as set on every RS row 3(**4**:4:**5**:5:**5**) times. *45(**48**:50:**52**:54:**56**) sts.*

Work straight in st st until armhole measures 4(**4¼**:4¼:**4¼**:4½:**4¾**)in/10(**11**:11:**11**:11.5:**12**)cm, ending with a WS row.

NECK SHAPING

Next row (RS): Bind (cast) off 10(**11**:11:**11**:12:**12**) sts, k to end. *35(**37**:39:**41**:42:**44**) sts.*

Next row: P.

Next row: Bind (cast) off 3 sts, k to end. *32(**34**:36:**38**:39:**41**) sts.*

Next row: P.

Next row: Ssk, k to end. *31(**33**:35:**37**:38:**40**) sts.*

Next row: P.

Cont to dec as set on every RS row 8(**8**:8:**10**:8:**10**) times, then on every foll 4th row 1(**1**:2:**1**:3:**2**) times. *22(**24**:25:**26**:27:**28**) sts.*

Work straight in st st until armhole measures 7(**7½**:8:**8**:8½:**8¾**)in/18(**19**:20:**20**:21.5:**22**)cm, ending with a RS row

Next row: Bind (cast) off 7(**8**:8:**9**:9:**9**) sts, p to end.

Next row: K.

Next row: Bind (cast) off 7(**8**:8:**9**:9:**9**) sts, p to end.

Next row: K.

Bind (cast) off rem 8(**8**:9:**8**:9:**10**) sts.

BACK

With RS facing, rejoin yarn to 109(**116**:122:**129**:135:**142**) sts left on holder, leaving 53(**57**:60:**63**:66:**69**) sts for left front.

ARMHOLE SHAPING

Bind (cast) off 4(**4**:5:**5**:6:**7**) sts at beg of next two rows. *101(**108**:112:**119**:123:**128**) sts.*

Next row: Ssk, k to last 2 sts, k2tog. *99(**106**:110:**117**:121:**126**) sts.*

Next row: P.

Cont to dec as set on every RS row 3(**4**:4:**5**:5:**5**) times. *93(**98**:102:**107**:111:**116**) sts.*

Work straight in st st until armhole matches right front to shoulder bind (cast) off, ending with a WS row.

NECK SHAPING

Next row: Bind (cast) off 7(**8**:8:**9**:9:**9**) sts, k15(**16**:17:**17**:18:**19**), k2tog, turn and work on these sts only.

Next row: P16(**17**:18:**18**:19:**20**).

Next row: Bind (cast) off 7(**8**:8:**9**:9:**9**) sts, k to end last two sts, k2tog.

Bind (cast) off rem 8(**8**:9:**8**:9:**10**) sts.

With RS facing, rejoin yarn to rem back sts and bind (cast) off 45(**46**:48:**51**:53:**56**) sts, k to end.

Next row: Bind (cast) off 7(**8**:8:**9**:9:**9**) sts, p to end.

Next row: Ssk, k to end.

Next row: Bind (cast) off 7(**8**:8:**9**:9:**9**) sts, p to end.

Next row: Ssk, k to end.

Bind (cast) off rem 8(**8**:9:**8**:9:**10**) sts.

LEFT FRONT

With RS facing, rejoin yarn to 53(**57**:60:**63**:66:**69**) sts left on holder.

ARMHOLE SHAPING

Next row: Bind (cast) off 4(**4**:5:**5**:6:**7**) sts, k to end. *49(**53**:55:**58**:60:**62**) sts.*

Next row: P.

Next row: Ssk, k to end. *48(**52**:54:**57**:59:**61**) sts.*

Next row: P.

Cont to dec as set on every RS row 3(**4**:4:**5**:5:**5**) times. *45(**48**:50:**52**:54:**56**) sts.*

Work straight in st st until armhole measures 4(**4¼**:4¼:**4¼**:4½:**4¾**)in/10(**11**:11:**11**:11.5:**12**)cm, ending with a RS row.

NECK SHAPING

Next row (WS): Bind (cast) off 10(**11**:11:**11**:12:**12**) sts, p to end. *35(**37**:39:**41**:42:**44**) sts.*

Next row: K.

Next row: Bind (cast) off 3 sts, p to end. *32(**34**:36:**38**:39:**41**) sts.*

Next row: K to last 2 sts, k2tog. *31(**33**:35:**37**:38:**40**) sts.*

Next row: P.

Cont to dec as set on every RS row 8(**8**:8:**10**:8:**10**) times and then on every foll 4th row 1(**1**:2:**1**:3:**2**) times. *22(**24**:25:**26**:27:**28**) sts.*

Work straight in st st until armhole matches back to shoulder bind (cast) off, ending with a RS row.

Next row: Bind (cast) off 7(**8**:8:**9**:9:**9**) sts, k to end.

Next row: P.

Next row: Bind (cast) off 7(**8**:8:**9**:9:**9**) sts, k to end.

Bind (cast) off rem 8(**8**:9:**8**:9:**10**) sts.

SLEEVES

Using US size 2 (2.75mm) needles cast on 55(**55**:59:**59**:65:**65**) sts.

Row 1: [K1, p1] seed (moss) st to last st, k1.

Rep Row 1 three more times.

Change to US size 2/3 (3mm) needles and cont in st st, starting with a k row.

Work straight for 10(**10**:10:**12**:8:**12**) rows.

Next row: K1, M1, k to last st, M1, k1. *57(**57**:61:**61**:67:**67**) sts.*

Cont to inc as set on every foll 12th(**12th**:14th:**12th**:14th:**12th**) row to 77(**79**:81:**83**:89:**91**) sts.

Work straight until sleeve measures 17¼(**17¾**:18:**18**:18½:**19**)in/44(**45**:46:**46**:47:**48**)cm.

SHAPE SLEEVE TOP

Bind (cast) off 4(**4**:5:**5**:6:**7**) sts at beg of next two rows. *69(**71**:71:**73**:77:**77**) sts.*

Next row: Ssk, k to last 2 sts, k2tog. *67(**69**:69:**71**:75:**75**) sts.*

Next row: P.

Cont to dec as set on every RS row 17(**18**:20:**21**:21:**23**) times, then on every row 3(**3**:1:**1**:3:**1**) times. *27 sts.*

Bind (cast) off 3 sts at beg of foll 4 rows. *15 sts.*

Bind (cast) off rem 15 sts.

NECKBAND

Join shoulder seams

With RS facing, using US size 2 (2.75mm) needles, pick up and k 13(**14**:14:**14**:15:**15**) sts across bound (cast) off sts on right front, 18(**18**:21:**21**:24:**24**) sts up right front, 4 sts down side neck, 43(**45**:47:**49**:51:**55**) sts evenly across back neck bind (cast) off, 4 sts up side neck, 18(**18**:21:**21**:24:**24**) sts down left front, 13(**14**:14:**14**:15:**15**) sts across bound (cast) off sts on left front. *113(**117**:125:**127**:137:**141**) sts.*

Row 1: [K1, p1] seed (moss st) to last st, k1.

Rep Row 1 three more times.

Bind (cast) off.

LEFT FRONT BUTTON BAND

With RS facing, using US size 2 (2.75mm) needles, pick up and k 111(**113**:111:**117**:113:**119**) sts evenly along left front and neck band edges.

Row 1: [K1, p1] seed (moss) st to last st, k1.

Rep Row 1 three more times.

Bind (cast) off.

RIGHT FRONT BUTTONHOLE BAND

With RS facing, using US size 2 (2.75mm) needles, pick up and k 111(**113**:111:**117**:113:**119**) sts evenly along right front and neck band edges.

Row 1: [K1, p1] seed (moss) st to last st, k1.

Row 2: [K1, p1] 41(**40**:39:**42**:39:**42**) times, k0(**1**:1:**0**:0:**0**), work 2 tog, yo, *work 6(**7**:7:**7**:8:**8**) sts in seed (moss) st as set, work 2 tog, yo, rep from * twice more, work in seed (moss) st to end.

Rep Row 1 twice more.

Bind (cast) off.

FINISHING

Join sleeve seams.

Set into body of cardigan.

Weave in all ends and sew buttons to left front button band.

salcombe shawl with pompoms

A lovely shawl or giant scarf with the perfect color combination to brighten up those cold winter months. It's worked from the point up, in a triangular shape.

SKILL RATING ● ● ●

MATERIALS

Scarf
Caron Big Cakes (100% acrylic, approx. 603yds/551m per 10½oz/300g ball) worsted (aran) weight yarn
  2 balls of 26018 Summer Berry Tart

Tassels
Caron Simply Soft (100% acrylic, approx. 314yds/228m per 6oz/170g ball) worsted (aran) weight yarn
  1 ball each of:
    0015 Strawberry (peach)
    9785 Baby Sunshine (yellow)
    9739 Soft Green (blue/green)

US size 8 (5mm) circular knitting needle, 48in (120cm) long

Yarn sewing needle

Pompom maker (optional)

FINISHED MEASUREMENT
Approx. 66½in (168cm) at widest point x 30in (76cm) long

GAUGE (TENSION)
14 sts x 28 rows over a 4in (10cm) square in garter stitch, using US size 8 (5mm) needles.

ABBREVIATIONS
approx.	approximately
cont	continue
k	knit
k2tog	knit 2 stitches together
patt	pattern
rem	remain
rep	repeat
st(s)	stitch(es)
yo	yarn over
[ ]	repeat sequence between square brackets the number of times stated

NOTE
Even though the shawl is worked in rows, it's best to use a circular needle because after a while you will have a large number of stitches.

FOR THE SHAWL
Cast on 5 sts.
Row 1: K1, yo, k1, yo, k1, yo, k1, yo, k1. *9 sts.*
Row 2 and all even rows: K.
Row 3: [K1, yo, k3, yo] twice, k1. *13 sts.*
Row 5: [K1, yo, k5, yo] twice, k1. *17 sts.*
Row 7: [K1, yo, k7, yo] twice, k1. *21 sts.*
Rows 8–17: Cont in patt as set, inc number of sts between pairs of yo in square brackets by 2 on each odd-number row. *41 sts.*
Row 18: K.
Row 19 (eyelet row): K1, yo, [k2tog, yo] 9 times, k1, yo, k1, yo, k1, [yo, k2tog] 9 times, yo, k1.
Row 20: K.
[Rep Rows 1–20 in patt as set] 5 times, making sure to keep the edge patterns and center patterns in line on eyelet rows.
Rep Rows 1–18 in patt as set.
Bind (cast) off loosely and fasten off.

FINISHING
Sew in any loose ends.

Make three pompoms, one in each color, and attach one to each corner.

mini dress

A great little dress to wear over jeans, leggings, or tights. It has a lovely shape and is straightforward to knit in stockinette (stocking) stitch.

SKILL RATING ● ● ●

MATERIALS

Sirdar Colourwheel (80% acrylic, 20% wool, approx. 568yds/520m per 5¼oz/150g ball) light worsted (DK) weight yarn
  10:**11**:12:**13**:14 balls of 203 Flower Garden

US size 3 (3.25mm) and US size 6 (4mm) knitting needles

2 stitch holders

Yarn sewing needle

1 button

GAUGE (TENSION)

22 sts x 28 rows over a 4in (10cm) square in stockinette (stocking) stitch, using US size 6 (4mm) needles.

FINISHED MEASUREMENTS

To fit

US size:	6	**8–10**	12–14	**14–16**	16–18
UK Size:	8	**10–12**	14–16	**16–18**	18–20
Bust:	30–31½	**33–34½**	36¼–38	**41–43¼**	43¼–45¾in
	76–80	**84–88**	92–97	**104–110**	110–116cm

ACTUAL MEASUREMENTS

Bust:	34	**38**	41¾	**46½**	51in
	86	**96**	106	**118**	130cm
Length:	30	**30¾**	32	**33**	34¼in
	76	**78**	81	**84**	87cm

ABBREVIATIONS

approx.	approximately	**rep**	repeat
beg	beginning	**RS**	RS
cont	continue	**sl1 k1 psso**	slip 1 stitch, knit 1 st, pass slipped stitch over
dec	decrease		
inc	increase	**st(s)**	stitch(es)
k	knit	**st st**	stockinette (stocking) stitch
k2tog	knit 2 stitches together		
M1	make 1 stitch	**y2rn**	wrap yarn around the needle twice
p	purl	**[ ]**	repeat sequence between square brackets the number of times stated
rem	remain		

FOR THE BACK

Using US size 3 (3.25mm) needles cast on 112(**122**:136:**152**:166) sts.
K 31 rows.
Change to US size 6 (4mm) needles.
Beg with a k row, cont in st st.
Work 10(**12**:12:**14**:14) rows.
Dec row: K10(**11**:12:**13**:14), sl1 k1 psso, k to last 12(**13**:14:**15**:16) sts, k2tog, k10(**11**:12:**13**:14).
Work 3 rows.
Rep the last 4 rows until there are 76(**86**:96:**110**:122) sts.

Cont straight until back measures 16(**16½**:17¼:**18**:19)in/41(**42**:44:**46**:48)cm from cast-on edge, ending with a p row.
Next row: K4(**5**:6:**7**:8), M1, k to last 4(**5**:6:**7**:8) sts, M1, k4(**5**:6:**7**:8).
Work 3 rows.
Rep the last 4 rows until there are 90(**106**:118:**130**:144) sts.
Cont straight until Back measures 22½(**23**:23½:**24½**:25)in/57(**58**:60:**62**:64)cm from cast-on edge, ending with a p row.

SHAPE ARMHOLES

Bind (cast) off 5(**5**:6:**6**:6) sts at beg of next 2 rows.
Dec one st at each end of next row and every foll alt
row until 80(**86**:92:**98**:104) sts rem.
Cont in st st until back measures 29(**30**:31:**32¼**:33½)
in/74(**76**:79:**82**:85)cm from cast-on edge, ending with
a p row.

SHAPE BACK NECK

Next row: K25(**27**:29:**31**:33) sts, turn and work on
these sts for first side of neck shaping.
Dec one st at neck edge on next 4 rows.
*21(**23**:25:**27**:29) sts.*
Work 1 row.

SHAPE SHOULDER

Bind (cast) off 10(**11**:12:**13**:14) sts at beg of next row.
Work 1 row.
Bind (cast) off rem 11(**12**:13:**14**:15) sts.
Slip center 30(**32**:34:**36**:38) sts on a holder, rejoin yarn
to rem sts, k to end.
Dec one st at neck edge on next 4 rows.
*21(**23**:25:**27**:29) sts.*
Work 2 rows.

SHAPE SHOULDER

Bind (cast) off 10(**11**:12:**13**:14) sts at beg of next row.
Work 1 row.
Bind (cast) off rem 11(**12**:13:**14**:15) sts.

FOR THE FRONT

Work as given for back until front measures
22½(**23**:23½:**24½**:25)in/57(**58**:60:**62**:64)cm from
cast-on edge, ending with a purl row.

SHAPE ARMHOLES

Bind (cast) off 5(**5**:6:**6**:6) sts at beg of next 2 rows.
Dec one st at each end of next row and every foll alt
row until 80(**86**:92:**98**:104) sts rem.
Cont in st st until front measures 29(**30**:31:**32¼**:33½)
in/74(**76**:79:**82**:85)cm from cast-on edge, ending with
a p row.

SHAPE FRONT NECK

K30(**32**:34:**36**:38)sts, turn and work on these sts for
first side of neck shaping. Dec one st at neck edge on
next 4 rows and every foll alt row until 21(**23**:25:**27**:29)
sts rem.

SHAPE SHOULDER

Bind (cast) off 10(**11**:12:**13**:14) sts at beg of next row.
Work one row.
Bind (cast) off rem 11(**12**:13:**14**:15) sts.
Slip center 20(**22**:24:**26**:28) sts on a holder, rejoin yarn to
rem sts, k to end.
Dec one st at neck edge on next 4 rows and every foll alt
row until 21(**23**:25:**27**:29)sts rem.
Work 2 rows.

SHAPE SHOULDER

Bind (cast) off 10(**11**:12:**13**:14) sts at beg of next row.
Work 1 row.
Bind (cast) off rem 11(**12**:13:**14**:15) sts.

FOR THE SLEEVES

Using US size 3 (3.25mm) needles cast on 66(**68**:72:**74**:76) sts.
K 31 rows.
Change to US size 6 (4mm) needles.
Beg with a k row, cont in st st.
Work 2 rows.
Dec row: K6, sl1 k1 psso, k to last 8 sts, k2tog, k6.
Work 15 rows.
Rep the last 16 rows 3 times more. 58(**60**:64:**66**:68) sts.
Inc row: K3, M1, k to last 3 sts, M1, k3.
Work 7 rows.
Rep the last 8 rows until there are 68(**70**:74:**76**:78) sts.
Cont straight until sleeve measures 17(**17**:17¼:**17¼**:17¾) in/43(**43**:44:**44**:45)cm from cast-on edge, ending with a p row.

SHAPE SLEEVE TOP
Bind (cast) off 5(**5**:6:**6**:6) sts at beg of next 2 rows.
Next row: K2, sl1 k1 psso, k to last 4 sts, k2tog, k2.
Next row: P to end.
Dec in this way at each end of the next 7(**8**:9:**10**:11) RS rows.
Work 7 rows straight.
Dec one st at each end of the next 3 RS rows.
Bind (cast) off 2 sts at beg of next 10 rows.
Bind (cast) off.

FOR THE LEFT NECKBAND

Using US size 3 (3.25mm) needles, pick up and k 17 sts down left side of front neck, turn, cast on 7 sts. 24 sts.
K 15 rows.
Bind (cast) off.

FOR THE RIGHT NECKBAND

Join right shoulder seam.
With US size 3 (3.25mm) needles, k across 20(**22**:24:**26**:28) sts from center front holder, pick up and k 17 sts up RS of front neck, 7 sts down RS of back neck, k across 30(**32**:34:**36**:38) sts from back neck holder, pick up and k 7 sts up left side of back neck. 81(**85**:89:**93**:97) sts.
K 7 rows.
Buttonhole row 1: K2, k2tog, y2rn, sl1 k1 psso, k to end.
Buttonhole row 2: K to end, working twice into y2rn.
K 6 rows.
Bind (cast) off.

FINISHING

Join left shoulder and neckband seam.
Join side and sleeve seams.
Set in sleeves.
Sew in any yarn ends.

crew-neck sweater

This is the ideal comfort garment; a lovely, chunky, and easy-to-knit sweater, perfect for cozy winter days.

MATERIALS

Caron Sprinkle Cakes (20% wool, 77% acrylic, approx. 204yds/186m per 8½oz/240g ball) super bulky (super chunky) weight yarn
  3 balls of 21003 Birthday Cake

US size 10½ (7mm) and US size 11 (8mm) straight knitting needles

US size 10½ (7mm) circular knitting needle, 24in (60cm) long

Yarn sewing needle

GAUGE (TENSION)

11 sts x 14 rows over a 4in (10cm) square in stockinette (stocking) stitch, using US size 11 (8mm) needles.

FINISHED MEASUREMENTS:

To fit						
US size:	6	**8**	10	**12**	14	**16**
UK size:	8	**10**	12	**14**	16	**18**
ACTUAL MEASUREMENTS						
Bust:	35¾	**37¼**	40	**41½**	43½	**45¾in**
	91	**94.5**	102	**105.5**	111	**116cm**
Length:	23½	**23¾**	24	**24¼**	24½	**24¾in**
	59.5	**60**	61	**61.5**	62	**62.5cm**

ABBREVIATIONS

alt	alternate	**patt**	pattern
approx.	approximately	**rep**	repeat
beg	begin	**RH**	right hand
cont	continue	**RS**	right side
dec	decreas(e)ing	**ssk**	slip 1 kwise, slip 1 kwise,
foll	follow(ing)		k2tog through back of loop
inc	increase	**st(s)**	stitch(es)
k	knit	**st st**	stockinette (stocking) stitch
k2tog	knit 2 stitches together	**WS**	wrong side
M1	make 1 stitch	**[ ]**	repeat sequence between
p	purl		square brackets the number
p2tog	purl 2 stitches together		of times stated

FOR THE BACK

Using US size 10½ (7mm) straight needles, cast on 50(**54**:58:**58**:62:**66**) sts.
Row 1: K2, [p2, k2] rib to end.
Row 2: P2, [k2, p2] rib to end.
Cont in rib until work measures 2½in (6cm) ending with a WS row.
Change to US size 11 (8mm) straight needles, work st st beg with a k row.

US SIZES 6 AND 12 (UK SIZES 8 AND 14) ONLY
Next row: K16(–:–:**18**:–:–), M1, k18(–:–:**22**:–:–), M1, k to end. *52(–:–:**60**:–:–) sts.*

US SIZE 14 (UK SIZE 16) ONLY
Next row: K31, M1, k to end. *63 sts.*

ALL OTHER SIZES
Next row: K to end.

ALL SIZES

Work 7 rows.

Next row: K1, ssk, k to last 3 sts, k2tog, k1. *50(**52**:56:**58**:61:**64**) sts.*

Work 9 rows.

Next row: K1, ssk, k to last 3 sts, k2tog, k1. *48(**50**:54:**56**:59:**62**) sts.*

Work 7(**7**:7:**5**:5:**5**) rows.

Next row: K1, M1, k to last st, M1, k1. *50(**52**:56:**58**:61:**64**) sts.*

Work 9 rows.

Next row: K1, M1, k to last st, M1, k1. *52(**54**:58:**60**:63:**66**) sts.*

Cont until work measures 16¼(**15¾**:15¼:**15¼**:15¼:**15**)in/ 41(**40**:39:**39**:39:**38**)cm from cast-on edge, finishing with a WS row.

SHAPE ARMHOLE

Bind (cast) off 2(**2**:3:**3**:3:**3**) sts at beg of next two rows. *48(**50**:52:**54**:57:**58**) sts.*

Dec 1 st at each end of next and foll 2(**2**:2:**2**:3:**3**) alt rows. *42(**44**:46:**48**:49:**50**) sts.*

Cont in patt until armhole measures 7½(7¾**:8½:**8¾**:9¼:**9¾**)in/19(**20**:21.5:**22**:23.5:**24.5**)cm from beg of shaping, ending with a WS row.

SHAPE SHOULDERS

Next row: Bind (cast) off 6(**6**:6:**6**:7:**7**) sts at beg of next row, k until 6(**6**:7:**7**:7:**7**) sts rem on RH needle, turn.

Next row: Dec 1 st, p to end. *5(**5**:6:**6**:6:**6**) sts.*

Bind (cast) off rem 5(**5**:6:**6**:6:**6**) sts.

Rejoin yarn to rem sts with RS facing and bind (cast) off 18(**20**:20:**22**:21:**22**) sts, k to end.

Complete left shoulder to match right, reversing shaping.

FOR THE FRONT

Work as back until **.

Cont straight until armhole measures 3½(**4**:4¼:**4¼**:4½:**5**)in/9(**10**:11:**11**:11.5:**12.5**)cm from beg of shaping ending with a WS row. *42(**44**:46:**48**:49:**50**) sts.*

START NECK SHAPING

Next row: K17(**18**:18:**19**:19:**19**), bind (cast) off 8(**8**:10:**10**:11:**12**) sts, k to end.

Dec 1 st at neck edge on next and foll 0(**3**:3:**3**:0:**0**) rows, and then on each RS row to 11(**11**:12:**12**:13:**13**) sts.

Cont straight until armhole matches back to shoulder shaping, finishing on a RS row.

SHAPE SHOULDERS

Next row: Bind (cast) off 6(**6**:6:**6**:7:**7**) sts, p to end. *5(**5**:6:**6**:6:**6**) sts.*

Bind (cast) off rem 5(**5**:6:**6**:6:**6**) sts.

With WS facing, rejoin yarn to rem sts, p2tog, p to end.

Complete left shoulder to match RH side, reversing all shaping.

FOR THE SLEEVE

Using US size 10½ (7mm) straight needles cast on 26(**26**:26:**30**:30:**30**) sts.

Row 1: K2, [p2, k2] rib to end.

Row 2: P2, [k2, p2] rib to end.

Cont in rib until work measures 2½in (6cm), ending with a WS row.

Change to US size 11 (8mm) straight needles, work st st beg with a k row.

Inc 1 st at each end of 5th(**3rd**:5th:**5th**:5th:**5th**) row and every foll 4th row to 28(**28**:32:**34**:38:**42**) sts, and then every 6th row to 40(**42**:44:**46**:48:**50**) sts.

Work straight until sleeve measures 17¾(**17¾**:18:**18**:18½:**18½**)in/45(**45**:46:**46**:47:**47**)cm from cast-on edge.

SHAPE SLEEVE CAP

Bind (cast) off 2(**2**:3:**3**:3:**3**) sts at beg of next two rows. *36(**38**:38:**40**:42:**44**) sts.*

Dec 1 st at each end of next and foll 1(**1**:2:**3**:6:**10**) alt rows. *32(**34**:32:**32**:28:**22**) sts.*

Dec 1 st at each end of foll 9(**10**:9:**9**:7:**3**) rows. *14(**14**:14:**14**:14:**16**) sts.*

Bind (cast) off 2 sts at beg of next 2 rows, then bind (cast) off rem 10(**10**:10:**10**:10:**12**) sts.

FOR THE NECKBAND

Join both shoulder seams.

With RS facing, using US size 10½ (7mm) circular needle, pick up and k 11(**12**:11:**12**:12:**13**) sts down left front neck, 8(**8**:10:**10**:11:**12**) sts from center front, 11(**12**:11:**12**:12:**13**) sts up right front neck, 2 sts from right back side, 18(**20**:20:**22**:21:**22**) sts from center back and 2 sts from left back side. *52(**56**:56:**60**:60:**64**) sts.*

Join to work in the round.

Next round: [K2, p2] rib to end.

Cont in rib until neckband measures 2in (5cm).

Starting with a k row, work 6 rows in st st.

Bind (cast) off.

FINISHING

Block and sew in any yarn ends.

Join side and sleeve seams, sew in sleeves.

roll-neck sweater

This really cozy item is great for both women and men. The intricate textures of the pattern show up really well against the gradient of the colors as they unwind from your needles.

SKILL RATING ● ● ●

MATERIALS

Caron Cakes (100% acrylic, approx. 382yds/350m per 7oz/200g ball) worsted (aran) weight yarn
4(**4**:**4**:**4**:**5**:**4**:**4**:**5**:**5**) balls of 17033 Blueberry Muffin

US size 6 (4mm) and US size 7 (4.5mm) straight knitting needles

US size 6 (4mm) circular needle, 16in (40cm) long

Stitch markers

Cable needle

Yarn sewing needle

FINISHED MEASUREMENTS

To fit

US lady's size:	6	**8**	10	**12**	14	**16**				
UK lady's size:	8	**10**	12	**14**	16	**18**				
Man's size:							S	M	L	XL

ACTUAL MEASUREMENTS

Actual chest:	32	**36**	37½	**39½**	42½	**45½**	37½	**42½**	45¾	**49½in**
	81	**91**	95	**100**	108	**116.5**	95	**108**	116.5	**125cm**
Length:	25½	**26**	26½	**26½**	26½	**27¼**	26	**27¼**	27¾	**28in**
	64.5	**66**	67	**67**	67	**69**	66	**69**	70.5	**71cm**
Sleeve length :	18	**18¼**	18¼	**18½**	18½	**19**	18½	**19**	19	**19¼in**
	45.5	**46**	46	**47**	47	**48**	47	**48**	48	**49cm**

GAUGE (TENSION)

18 sts x 25 rows over a 4in (10cm) square in reverse stockinette (stocking) stitch, using US size 7 (4.5mm) needles.

ABBREVIATIONS

alt	alternate
approx.	approximately
beg	beginning
cont	continue
dec	decrease
foll	following
inc	increase
k	knit
M1	make 1 stitch
p	purl
patt	pattern
rem	remain

rep	repeat
rev st st	reverse stockinette (stocking) stitch
RS	right side
st(s)	stitch(es)
st st	stockinette (stocking) stitch
WS	wrong side
[ ]	repeat sequence between square brackets the number of times stated

SPECIAL ABBREVIATIONS

C5B: cable 5 back: sl next 3 sts onto cable needle, and hold to back, k2, k3 from cable needle
C5F: cable 5 front: sl next 2 sts onto cable needle, and hold in front, k3, k2 from cable needle
MB: make bobble: (K1, p1, k1, p1, k1, p1, k1) into one st, slip 2nd st on RH needle over first, rep for 3rd, 4th, 5th 6th and 7th sts

Tw5R: twist 5 right: slip next 3 sts onto cable needle, and hold to back, k2, then p1, k2 from cable needle
Tw3R: twist 3 right: slip next 1 st onto cable needle and hold to back, k2, then p1 from cable needle
Tw3L: twist 3 left: slip next 2 sts onto cable needle and hold to front, p1, then k2 from cable needle

CABLE PATT 1: BOBBLE TWIST RIGHT

Worked over 5 sts.

Row 1: C5B.

Row 2 and all WS rows: P.

Row 3: K5.

Row 5: K2, MB, k2.

Row 7: K5.

Row 8: P.

CABLE PATT 2: BOBBLE TWIST LEFT

Worked over 5 sts.

Row 1: C5F.

Rows 2–8: As for Cable patt 1.

CABLE PATT 3: HALF DIAMOND CABLE WITH BOBBLES

Worked over 19 sts.

Row 1: P7, Tw5R, p7.

Row 2: K7, p2, k1, p2, k7.

Row 3: P6, Tw3R, p1, Tw3L, p6.

Row 4: K6, p2, k3, p2, k6.

Row 5: P5, Tw3R, p1, MB, p1, Tw3L, p5.

Row 6: K5, p2, k5, p2, k5.

Row 7: P4, Tw3R, [p1, MB] twice, p1, Tw3L, p4.

Row 8: K4, p2, k7, p2, k4.

Row 9: P3, Tw3R, [p1, MB] 3 times, p1, Tw3L, p3.

Row 10: K3, p2, k9, p2, k3.

Row 11: P2, Tw3R, p2, k2, p1, k2, p2, Tw3L, p2.

Row 12: K2, p2, k3, p2, k1, p2, k3, p2, k2.

Row 13: P1, Tw3R, p3, k2, p1, k2, p3, Tw3L, p1.

Row 14: K7, p2, k1, p2, k7.

FOR THE BACK

Cast on 82(**90**:94:**98**:106:**114**:94:**106**:114:**122**) sts using US size 7 (4.5mm) straight needles.

Row 1: [K2, p2] rib to last 2 sts, k2.

Row 2: [P2, k2] rib to last 2 sts, p2.

Cont in rib as set for 11 more rows

Row 14: Rib 9(**13**:9:**11**:5:**9**:9:**5**:9:**13**), [M1, rib 8(**8**:10:**10**:10:**10**:10:**10**:10:**10**)] 2(**2**:2:**2**:3:**3**:2:**3**:3:**3**) times, M1, rib 16(**16**:18:**18**:18:**18**:18:**18**:18:**18**), M1, rib 16(**16**:18:**18**:18:**18**:18:**18**:18:**18**), M1, [rib 8(**8**:10:**10**:10:**10**:10:**10**:10:**10**), M1] 2(**2**:2:**2**:3:**3**:2:**3**:3:**3**) times, rib 9(**13**:9:**11**:5:**9**:9:**5**:9:**13**). 89(**97**:101:**105**:115:**123**:101:**115**:123:**131**) sts.

Next row (cable set up RS): P7(**11**:7:**9**:3:**7**:7:**3**:7:**11**), [work row 1 of cable patt 1, p4(**4**:6:**6**:6:**6**:6:**6**:6:**6**)] 3(**3**:3:**3**:4:**4**:3:**4**:4:**4**) times, p1, work row 1 of cable patt 3, p1, [p4(**4**:6:**6**:6:**6**:6:**6**:6:**6**), work row 1 of cable patt 2] 3(**3**:3:**3**:4:**4**:3:**4**:4:**4**) times, p7(**11**:7:**9**:3:**7**:7:**3**:7:**11**).

This row sets position of cable patts with rev st st (p RS rows, k WS rows) between. Cont as set until work measures 18(**18**:18:**17½**:17½:**17¼**:17:**17¾**:17¾:**17¾**)in/ 45.5(**45.5**:45.5:**44.5**:44.5:**43.5**:43:**45**:45:**45**)cm from cast-on edge, finishing with a WS row.

SHAPE ARMHOLES

Bind (cast) off 2(**3**:4:**4**:5:**6**:4:**5**:6:**7**) sts at beg of next two rows. *85(**91**:93:**97**:105:**111**:93:**105**:111:**117**) sts.*
Cont to work all sts as set by patt.
Dec 1 at each end of next and foll 2(**3**:2:**2**:2:**5**:1:**2**:3:**5**) alt rows. *79(**83**:87:**91**:99:**99**:89:**99**:103:**105**) sts.*
**Cont in patt until armhole measures
7½(**8**:8½:**8¾**:9:**10**:9:**9½**:10:**10¼**)in/19(**20**:21.5:**22**:23:**25**:23:**24**:25:**26**)cm from beg of shaping, ending with a WS row.

SHAPE SHOULDERS

Bind (cast) off 7(**7**:8:**8**:9:**9**:8:**8**:9:**10**) sts at beg of next two rows. *65(**69**:71:**75**:81:**81**:73:**83**:85:**85**) sts.*
Bind (cast) off 7(**7**:7:**8**:9:**9**:7:**9**:9:**9**) sts at beg of next two rows. *51(**55**:57:**59**:63:**63**:59:**65**:67:**67**) sts.*
Bind (cast) off 6(**7**:7:**8**:9:**9**:7:**9**:9:**9**) sts at beg of next two rows.
Bind (cast) off rem 39(**41**:43:**43**:45:**45**:45:**47**:49:**49**) sts.

FOR THE FRONT

Work as back to **.
Cont in patt until armhole measures
4(**4**:4¼:**4½**:4¾:**5**:4¾:**5**:5:**5½**)in/10(**10**:11:**11.5**:12:**13**:12:**13**:13:**14**)cm from beg of shaping, ending with WS row.

SHAPE NECK

Next row: Patt 31(**33**:35:**36**:40:**40**:35:**40**:41:**42**), bind (cast) off 17(**17**:17:**19**:19:**19**:19:**19**:21:**21**) sts, patt to end.
Working on right front neck sts only, dec 1 st at neck edge on next and foll 4(**4**:4:**4**:4:**4**:6:**6**:6:**6**) rows, and then on each alt row to 20(**21**:22:**24**:27:**27**:22:**26**:27:**28**) sts.
Cont straight until armhole matches back to shoulder shaping, finishing on a RS row.

SHAPE SHOULDER

Next row: Bind (cast) off 7(**7**:8:**8**:9:**9**:8:**8**:9:**10**) sts at beg of next row. *13(**14**:14:**16**:18:**18**:14:**18**:18:**18**) sts.*
Next row: K to end.
Next row: Bind (cast) off 7(**7**:7:**8**:9:**9**:7:**9**:9:**9**) sts at beg of next row. *6(**7**:7:**8**:9:**9**:7:**9**:9:**9**) sts.*
Next row: K to end.
Bind (cast) off rem 6(**7**:7:**8**:9:**9**:7:**9**:9:**9**) sts.
With WS facing, rejoin yarn to rem sts, p to end.
Complete left neck to match right, reversing all shaping.

FOR THE SLEEVES

Using US size 6 (4mm) straight needles cast on 38(**42**:42:**46**:46:**50**:42:**46**:50:**50**) sts.
Row 1: [K2, p2] rib to last 2 sts, k2.
Row 2: [P2, k2] rib to last 2 sts, p2.
Cont in rib as set for 13 more rows
Row 16: Rib 3(**5**:3:**5**:5:**7**:3:**5**:7:**7**), M1, rib 16(**16**:18:**18**:18:**18**:18:**18**:18:**18**), M1, rib 16(**16**:18:**18**:18:**18**:18:**18**:18:**18**), M1, rib 3(**5**:3:**5**:5:**7**:3:**5**:7:**7**). *41(**45**:45:**49**:49:**53**:45:**49**:53:**53**) sts.*
Change to US size 7 (4.5mm) needles
Next row (cable set up RS): P1(**3**:1:**3**:3:**5**:1:**3**:5:**5**), work row 1 of cable patt 1, p5(**5**:7:**7**:7:**7**:7:**7**:7:**7**), work row 1 of cable patt 3, p5(**5**:7:**7**:7:**7**:7:**7**:7:**7**), work row 1 of cable patt 2, p1(**3**:1:**3**:3:**5**:1:**3**:5:**5**).
This row sets position of cable patts with rev st st between. Work 3 rows.
Inc 1 st at each end of next and foll 4th row until 55(**57**:73:**77**:85:**87**:73:**85**:87:**93**) sts, then on every 6th row until 73(**77**:83:**87**:91:**95**:83:**91**:95:**99**) sts.
AT SAME TIME when once you have 4(**4**:6:**6**:6:**6**:6:**6**:6:**6**) sts in rev st st at each end, work next 5 inc sts in st st to rep the same cable and bobble panel at each side. Work rem inc sts in rev st st.
Work straight until sleeve measures 18(**18¼**:18¼:**18½**:18½:**19**:18½:**19**:19:**19¼**)in/46(**46.5**:46.5:**47**:47:**48**:47:**48**:48:**49**)cm from cast-on edge.

SHAPE SLEEVE CAP

Bind (cast) off 2(**3**:4:**4**:5:**6**:4:**5**:6:**7**) sts at beg of next two rows. *69(**71**:75:**79**:81:**83**:75:**81**:83:**85**) sts.*
Dec 1 st at each end of next and foll 4(**5**:5:**5**:6:**7**:3:**4**:5:**6**) alt rows. *59(**59**:63:**67**:67:**67**:67:**71**:71:**71**) sts.*
Dec 1 st at each end of next 3(**3**:5:**7**:7:**7**:7:**9**:9:**9**) rows.
Bind (cast) off 6 sts at beg of next 6 rows.
Bind (cast) off rem 17 sts.

FOR THE NECKBAND

Join both shoulder seams.
With RS facing, using US size 6 (4mm) circular needle, pick up and k 17(**18**:19:**20**:21:**23**:19:**20**:22:**22**) sts down left front neck, 16(**16**:16:**18**:18:**18**:18:**18**:20:**20**) sts from center front, 17(**18**:19:**20**:21:**23**:19:**20**:22:**22**) sts up right front neck, 38(**40**:42:**42**:44:**44**:44:**46**:48:**48**) sts from center back. *88(**92**:96:**100**:104:**108**:100:**104**:112:**112**) sts.*
Place marker for start of round.
Work in the round in (k2, p2) rib until neckband measures 11in (28cm).
Bind (cast) off in rib.

FINISHING

Join side and sleeve seams and sew in the sleeves.

Block to size and sew in any yarn ends.

collar cardigan

This is a stockinette (stocking) stitch cardigan, which is a simple garment to knit, but it has a collar that gives it a bit of knitting style!

SKILL RATING ● ● ●

MATERIALS

Schoppel Wolle Gradient (100% wool, approx. 284yds/260m per 3½oz/100g ball) light worsted (DK) weight yarn
4(**4**:5:**5**) balls of 2336 Woman in the Woods

US size 4 (3.5mm) and US size 6 (4mm) knitting needles

3 stitch holders

Yarn sewing needle

9 buttons

GAUGE (TENSION)

22 sts x 30 rows over a 4in (10cm) square in stockinette (stocking) st, using US size 6 (4mm) needles.

FINISHED MEASUREMENTS

To fit bust:	32–34	**36–38**	40–42	**44–46in**
	82–86	**91–97**	102–107	**112–117cm**
ACTUAL MEASUREMENTS				
Bust:	36	**40**	45	**49½in**
	91	**102**	114.5	**125.5cm**
Length to shoulder:	19¾	**20**	20½	**21in**
	50	**51**	52	**53cm**
Sleeve length:	18½	**19**	19¼	**19¼in**
	47	**48**	49	**49cm**

ABBREVIATIONS

approx.	approximately	**rib 2 tog**	rib 2 sts togther
beg	beginning	**RS**	right side
cont	continue	**sl2 k1 p2sso**	slip 2 stitches, knit 1
dec	decrease		stitch, pass 2 slipped
foll	following		stitches over
inc	increase	**st(s)**	stitch(es)
k	knit	**st st**	stockinette (stocking)
k2tog	knit 2 stitches together		stitch
M1	make 1 stitch	**WS**	wrong side
p	purl	**yrn**	yarn round needle
rem	remain	**[ ]**	repeat sequence
rep	repeat		between square
			brackets the number
			of times stated

FOR THE BACK

Using US size 4 (3.5mm) needles, cast on 103(**115**:129:**14**1) sts.
Row 1: K1, [p1, k1] rib to end.
Row 2: P1, [k1, p1] rib to end.
Rep the last 2 rows 7 more times.
Change to US size 6 (4mm) needles.
Beg with a k row, cont in st st until work measures 12(**12**:11½:**11**)in/30(**30**:29:**28**)cm from cast-on edge, ending with a WS row.

SHAPE ARMHOLES

Bind (cast) off 4(**5**:6:**7**) sts at beg of next 2 rows. *95(**105**:117:**127**) sts.*
Dec one st at each end of the next 3(**5**:7:**9**) rows, then on foll 4(**6**:6:**7**) RS rows. *81(**83**:91:**95**) sts.*
Work straight until work measures 19¾(**20**:20½:**21**)in/ 50(**51**:52:**53**)cm from cast-on edge, ending with a WS row.

SHAPE SHOULDERS

Bind (cast) off 12(**12**:14:**14**) sts at beg of next 2 rows and 12(**12**:13:**14**) sts on foll 2 rows.
Leave rem 33(**35**:37:**39**) sts on st holder.

FOR THE LEFT FRONT

Using US size 4 (3.5mm) needles, cast on 50(**56**:63:**69**) sts.
Row 1: P0(**0**:1:**1**), [k1, p1] rib to end.
Row 2: [K1, p1] rib to last 0(**0**:1:**1**) st, k0(**0**:1:**1**).
Rep the last 2 rows 7 more times.
Change to US size 6 (4mm) needles.
Beg with a k row, cont in st st until work measures 12(**12**:11½:**11**)in/30(**30**:31:**31**)cm from cast-on edge, ending with a WS row.**

SHAPE ARMHOLE

Bind (cast) off 4(**5**:6:**7**) sts at beg of next row. *46(**51**:57:**62**) sts.*
P 1 row.
Dec one st at armhole edge of the next 3(5:7:9) rows, then on foll 4(**6**:6:**7**) RS rows. *39(**40**:44:**46**) sts.*
Work straight until work measures 17(**17¼**:17½:**18**)in/43(**44**:44.5:**45.5**)cm from cast-on edge, ending with a WS row.

SHAPE NECK

Next row: K to last 10(**11**:11:**12**) sts, turn, leaving rem sts on st holder. *29(**29**:33:**34**) sts.*
Next row: P to end.
Next row: K to last 2 sts, k2tog. *28(**28**:32:**33**) sts.*
Cont to dec one st at neck edge on every RS row until 24(24:27:**28**) sts rem.
Work straight until work measures same as back to shoulder shaping, ending with a WS row.

SHAPE SHOULDER

Next row: Bind (cast) off 12(**12**:14:**14**) sts, k to end.
P 1 row.
Bind (cast) off rem 12(**12**:13:**14**) sts.

FOR THE RIGHT FRONT

Using US size 4 (3.5mm) needles, cast on 50(**56**:63:**69**) sts.
Row 1: [P1, k1] rib to last 0(**0**:1:**1**) st, p0(**0**:1:**1**),
Row 2: K0(**0**:1:**1**), [p1, k1] rib to end.
These rows set rib, work as for left front to **, ending with a RS row.
Bind (cast) off 4(**5**:6:**7**) sts at beg of next row. *46(**51**:57:**62**) sts.*
Dec one st at armhole edge of the next 3(5:7:**9**) rows, then on foll 4(**6**:6:**7**) RS rows. *39(**40**:44:**46**) sts.*
Work straight until work measures 17(**17¼**:17½:**18**)in/43(**44**:44.5:**45.5**)cm from cast-on edge, ending with a RS row.

SHAPE NECK

Next row: P to last 10(**11**:11:**12**) sts, turn, leaving rem sts on st holder. *29(**29**:33:**34**) sts.*
Next row: K2tog, k to end. *28(**28**:32:**33**) sts.*
Cont to dec one st at neck edge on every RS row until 24(**24**:27:**28**) sts rem.
Work straight until work measures same as back to shoulder shaping, ending with a RS row.

SHAPE SHOULDER

Next row: Bind (cast) off 12(**12**:14:**14**) sts, p to end.
K 1 row.
Bind (cast) off rem 12(**12**:13:**14**) sts.

FOR THE SLEEVES

Using US size 4 (3.5mm) needles, cast on 45(**49**:57:**61**) sts.
Row 1: P1, [k1, p1] rib to end.
Row 2: K1, [p1, k1] rib to end.
Rep the last 2 rows 7 times more.
Change to US size 6 (4mm) needles.
Beg with a k row, cont in st st.
Work 6 rows.
Next row: K1, M1, k to last st, M1, k1. *47(**51**:59:**63**) sts.*
Cont to inc as set at each end of every foll 6th row 11(**14**:12:**15**) more times, and then on every 8th row to 77(**83**:91:**97**) sts.
Work straight until work measures 18½(**19**:19¼:**19¼**)in/47(**48**:49:**49**)cm from cast-on edge, ending with a WS row.

SHAPE TOP

Bind (cast) off 4(**5**:6:**7**) sts at beg of next 2 rows. *69(**73**:79:**83**) sts.*
Dec 1 st at each end of next and on foll 0(**0**:1:**2**) 4th rows. *67(**71**:75:**77**) sts.*
Dec 1 st at each end of 10(**10**:10:**11**) foll RS rows, and then on every row to 35(**35**:43:**43**) sts.
Bind (cast) off 2(**2**:3:**3**) sts at beg of next 4 rows.
Bind (cast) off rem 27(**27**:31:**31**) sts.

FOR THE NECKBAND

Join shoulder seams.
With RS facing, using US size 4 (3.5mm) needles, k 10(**11**:11:**12**) sts from right front neck holder, pick up and k 16(**16**:17:**17**) sts up right front neck, k33(**35**:37:**39**) sts from back neck holder, pick up and k 16(**16**:17:**17**) sts down left front neck, then k 10(**11**:11:**12**) sts from left front holder. *85(**89**:93:**97**) sts.*
Row 1: P1, [k1, p1] rib to end.
Row 2: K1, [p1, k1] rib to end.
Rep last 2 rows once more.
Bind (cast) off in rib.

tip

You may wish to steam the edge of the collar again once it is stitched in place.

FOR THE BUTTON BAND

With RS facing, US size 4 (3.5mm) needles, pick up and k 97(**99**:101:**103**) sts along left front edge.
Row 1: P1, [k1, p1] rib to end.
Row 2: K1, [p1, k1] rib to end.
Rep last 2 rows once more.
Bind (cast) off in rib.

FOR THE BUTTONHOLE BAND

With RS facing, US size 4 (3.5mm) needles, pick up and k 97(**99**:101:**103**) sts along right front edge.
Row 1: P1, [k1, p1] rib to end.
Buttonhole row: Rib 4(**6**:7:**2**), yrn, rib 2tog, [rib 9(**9**:9:**10**), yrn, rib 2tog] 8 times, rib to end.
Rib 2 rows.
Bind (cast) off in rib.

FOR THE COLLAR

Using US size 4 (3.5mm) needles, cast on 119(**123**:127:**131**) sts.
Row 1: K.
Row 2: K9, sl2 k1 p2sso, k to last 12 sts, sl2 k1 p2sso, k9.
Row 3: P to end.
Row 4: K8, sl2 k1 p2sso, k to last 11 sts, sl2 k1 p2sso, k8.
Row 5: P to end.
Cont in this way until foll row has been worked: K1, sl2 k1 p2sso, k to last 4 sts, sl2 k1 p2sso, k1. *83(**87**:91:**95**) sts*.
Next row: P to end.
Bind (cast) off 5 sts at beg of next 6(**6**:8:**8**) rows. *53(**57**:51:**55**) sts*.
Bind (cast) off.

FINISHING

Join side and sleeve seams, sew in sleeves.

Lightly steam the collar to flatten the edge. Join it around the neckband, ensuring that the RS of the collar is outward when the collar is folded back. Ease to fit and leave the front bands free.

Press the front bands and sew around the edge of the collar to keep in place onto the cardigan. Sew on the buttons.

lace shawl

If you like a challenge and appreciate the fineness of knitting in lace, then this is a most rewarding project. The stitch is absolutely beautiful and it looks stunning. Note the edging is knitted separately and sewn on to the main piece afterwards.

SKILL RATING ● ● ●

MATERIALS

Schoppel Wolle Zauberball 100 (100% wool, approx. 437yds/400m per 3½oz/100g ball) light fingering (3-ply) weight yarn
  4 balls of 2331 Comfort Zone

US size 5 (3.75mm) knitting needles

Yarn sewing needle

FINISHED MEASUREMENT

23¼in (59cm) wide x 67in (170cm) long after blocking

GAUGE (TENSION)

28 sts x 33 rows over a 4in (10cm) square in patt after blocking, using US size 5 (3.75mm) needles.

ABBREVIATIONS

approx.	approximately
beg	beginning
foll	follow(s)ing
k	knit
k2tog	knit 2 stitches together
p	purl
p2tog	purl 2 stitches together
patt	pattern
rem	remain
rep	repeat
RS	right side
sl1	slip 1 stitch
sl1 k1 psso	slip 1 stitch, knit 1 stitch, pass slipped stitch over
ssk	slip slip knit
st(s)	stitch(es)
tbl	through back of loop
WS	wrong side
yo	yarn over
[ ]	repeat sequence between square brackets the number of times stated

FOR THE SHAWL

Cast on 138 sts.

Row 1 (RS): K1, *k3, k2tog, k4, yo, p2, [k2, yo, ssk] 3 times, p2, yo, k4, ssk, k3; rep from * to last st, k1.

Row 2 (WS): K1, *p2, p2tog tbl, p4, yo, p1, k2, [p2, yo, p2tog] 3 times, k2, p1, yo, p4, p2tog, p2; rep from * to last st, k1.

Row 3 (RS): K1, *k1, k2tog, k4, yo, k2, p2, [k2, yo, ssk] 3 times, p2, k2, yo, k4, ssk, k1; rep from * to last st, k1.

Row 4: K1, *p2tog tbl, p4, yo, p3, k2, [p2, yo, p2tog] 3 times, k2, p3, yo, p4, p2tog; rep from * to last st, k1.

Rows 5–12: Rep Rows 1–4 twice more.

Row 13: K1, *yo, ssk, k2, yo, ssk, p2, yo, k4, ssk, k6, k2tog, k4, yo, p2, k2, yo, ssk, k2; rep from * to last st, k1.

Row 14: K1, *yo, p2tog, p2, yo, p2tog, k2, p1, yo, p4, p2tog, p4, p2tog tbl, p4, yo, p1, k2, p2, yo, p2tog, p2; rep from * to last st, k1.

Row 15: K1, *yo, ssk, k2, yo, ssk, p2, k2, yo, k4, ssk, k2, k2tog, k4, yo, k2, p2, k2, yo, ssk, k2; rep from * to last st, k1.

Row 16: K1, *yo, p2tog, p2, yo, p2tog, k2, p3, yo, p4, p2tog, p2tog tbl, p4, yo, p3, k2, p2, yo, p2tog, p2; rep from * to last st, k1.

Rows 17 to 24: Rep Rows 13–16 twice more.

Rows 1–24 form patt, rep them until work measures approx. 63in (160cm), ending on a Row 24.

Bind (cast) off.

FOR THE EDGING

Cast on 12 sts.
K 1 row.
Row 1 (RS): Sl1, k1, yo, k2tog, yo, k8.
Row 2: K13.
Row 3: Sl1, k1, yo, k2tog, k1, yo, k8.
Row 4: K14.
Row 5: Sl1, k1, [yo, k2tog] twice, yo, k8.
Row 6: K15.
Row 7: Sl1, k1, yo, k2tog, k1, yo, k2tog, yo, k8.
Row 8: K16.
Row 9: Sl1, k1, [yo, k2tog] 3 times, yo, k8.
Row 10: K17.
Row 11: Sl1, k1, yo, k2tog, k1, [yo, k2tog] twice, yo, k8.
Row 12: Bind (cast) off 6 sts, k to end. *12 sts.*
Rep Rows 1–12 until border is long enough to go around shawl, working last rep as foll:

Row 1: Sl1, k1, yo, k2tog, yo, k8.
Row 2: K13.
Row 3: Sl1, k1, yo, k2tog, k1, yo, k8.
Row 4: K14.
Row 5: Sl1, k1, [yo, k2tog] twice, yo, k8.
Row 6: K15.
Row 7: Sl1 k1 psso, yo, k2tog, k1, yo, k2tog, yo, k8.
Row 8: K15.
Row 9: Sl1 k1 psso, k1, [yo, k2tog] twice, yo, k8.
Row 10: K15.
Row 11: Sl1 k1 psso, k1, [yo, k2tog] twice, yo, k8.
Row 12: Bind (cast) off 6 sts, k to end. *9 sts.*
Bind (cast) off rem sts and join to cast-on edge at beg to complete corner.

FINISHING

Block and sew in any yarn ends.

tips

Keep a note of the rows using a row counter or your chosen method.

To make sure the edging is long enough, make enough to go around two sides but don't bind (cast) off. Pin and sew the edging onto the main piece, then continue to make edging until it goes right around the shawl.

women's socks

You can never have enough knitted socks and these make a fantastic gift. Sometimes the subtle changes of color block yarns work beautifully and these socks show this off really well. This is a basic pattern for socks made for an average-size woman's foot, but you can use the chart on page 91 as a guide to change the sizing.

you can use the chart on page 91 as a guide to change the sizing.

SKILL RATING ● ● ●

MATERIALS
Schoppel Wolle Zauberball 100 (100% wool, approx. 437yds/400m per 3½oz/100g ball) light fingering (3-ply) weight yarn
  1 ball of 2264 Light in the Tunnel

Set of 5 US size 2/3 (2.5mm) double-pointed needles

Stitch markers

Yarn sewing needle

FINISHED MEASUREMENT
To fit an average-size woman's foot

GAUGE (TENSION)
30 sts x 42 rows over a 4in (10cm) square in stockinette (stocking) stitch, using US size 2/3 (2.5mm) needles.

ABBREVIATIONS
approx.	approximately
beg	beginning
cont	continue
dec	decrease
k	knit
k2tog	knit 2 stitches together
p	purl
p2tog	purl 2 stitches together
rem	remain
rep	repeat
RS	right side
sl	slip
sl1 k1 psso	slip 1 stitch, knit 1 stitch, pass slipped stitch over
st(s)	stitch(es)
[ ]	repeat sequence between square brackets the number of times stated

FOR THE SOCKS
(make 2)

CUFF
Cast on 64 sts, 16 sts on each of 4 needles. Join into a round.
K 1 row.
Work in (k2, p2) rib for 16 rounds.

LEG
K 64 rounds.

HEEL FLAP
The heel is knitted in rows (k and p rows) over 32 sts.
Work on sts from needles 1 and 4. Leave sts on needles 3 and 2 till later.
Row 1: Using 4th needle, k16 sts (32 sts on needle), turn.
Place marker in center of these sts, between 16th and 17th st.
Cont working on these 32 sts.
Row 2: K2, p28, k2.
Row 3: K32.
Row 4: K2, p28, k2.
Rep Rows 3 and 4 for 32 rows.

tip

You can adjust the length of the foot using the chart on page 91.

You can adjust the length of the foot using the chart on page 91.

BEG DEC

Count 10 sts from each end of needle and place marker. There should be 10 sts at each end (end section) and 12 sts between markers (middle section).

Row 1 (RS): K21 (until last st of middle section), k2tog (last st of middle section and first st of the end section), turn.

Row 2: P11 (until last st of middle section), p2tog (last st of middle section and first st of the end section), turn.

Row 3: K11 (until last st of middle section), k2tog (last st of middle section and first st of the end section), turn.
Rep Rows 2 and 3 until only sts of middle section are left. *12 sts.*

GUSSET

Place marker after one half of heel sts to mark beg of round. *6 sts.*

Knit across heel sts.

With same needle (needle 1), pick up 16 sts between little knots up side. Pick up one extra st in corner before second needle. With next two needles, k across needles 2 and 3. *16 sts on each needle.*

Pick up one st in corner after third needle, then with next needle (needle 4) pick up another 16 sts between knots up next side.

Using same needle, knit 6 sts to st marker (start of next round).

Slip rem sts of heel onto needle 1.

Needles 1 and 4 should have 23 sts on each needle.

Place marker to denote beg of round between needles 1 and 4.

Needles 2 and 3 should have 16 sts on each needle.

GUSSET DEC

Knit one round.

Dec round: Needle 1: K to last 3 sts, k2tog, k1; Needles 2 and 3: K; Needle 4: K1, sl1 k1 psso, k to end.

Next 2 rounds: K.

Rep Dec round on 3rd round.

Rep last 3 rounds until 16 sts rem on each needle.

Cont straight until foot is long enough for required shoe size without toes.

CHART OF FOOT LENGTH (WITHOUT TOES)

		Approx. US shoe size	Approx. UK shoe size	Approx. European shoe size
7in	18cm	3–4	1–2	34–35
7½in	19cm	5–6	3–4	36–37
8in	20cm	7–8	5–6	38–39
8¼in	21cm	9–10	7–8	40–41

TOE

Dec round: Needle 1: K to last 3 sts, k2tog, k1; Needle 2: K1, sl1 k1 psso, k to end; Needle 3: K to last 3 sts, k2tog, k1; Needle 4: K1, sl1 k1 psso, k to end. *60 sts.*
Rounds 2–4: K.
Round 5: As Dec round. *56 sts.*
Rounds 6–7: K.
Round 8: As Dec round. *52 sts.*
Rounds 9–10: K.
Round 11: As Dec round. *48 sts.*
Round 12: K.

Round 13: As Dec round. *44 sts.*
Round 14: K.
Round 15: As Dec round. *40 sts.*
Round 16: K.
Round 17: As Dec round. *36 sts.*
Round 18: K.
Rounds 19–25: As Dec round. *8 sts (2 sts on each needle).*
Cut yarn and pull through rem sts.

FINISHING

Block and sew in any yarn ends.

for babies

baby lovies

These cute animal mini blankets are all the rage in the baby world. One ball of Bernat Softee Baby Stripes makes three blankies and three heads, but only just—I used up every scrap of yarn. If you run out of yarn the heads can easily be made using small amounts from your yarn stash.

SKILL RATING ● ● ○

MATERIALS:

Bernat Softee Baby Stripes (100% acrylic, approx. 286yds/262m per 4¼oz/120g ball) light worsted (DK) weight yarn
  1 ball of 53018 Wildflowers Stripe

Scrap of black yarn for embroidered face details

US size 6 (4mm) knitting needles

Set of 4 US size 6 (4mm) double-pointed needles

Stitch marker

Yarn sewing needle

Toy stuffing

FINISHED MEASUREMENTS

Approx. 8½ x 8½in (21.5 x 21.5cm)

GAUGE (TENSION)

Approx. 22 sts x 30 rows over a 4in (10cm) square in stockinette (stocking) stitch, using US size 6 (4mm) needles.

ABBREVIATIONS

approx.	approximately
beg	beginning
dec	decrease
inc	increase
k	knit
k2tog	knit 2 stitches together
kfb	knit into front and back of next stitch
M1	make 1 stitch
p	purl
p2tog	purl 2 stitches together
prev	previously
rem	remain(ing)
rep	repeat
RS	right side
sl1	slip 1 stitch
sl1 k2tog psso	slip 1 stitch, knit 2 stitches together, pass slipped stitch over
st(s)	stitch(es)
st st	stockinette (stocking) stitch
[ ]	repeat sequence between square brackets the number of times stated

FOR THE BLANKIES

(make 3)
Using US size 6 (4mm) needles, cast on 3 sts.
Row 1 (inc): Sl1, kfb in next st, k to end.
Rep Row 1 until there are 60 sts on needle.
Next row (dec): Sl1, k2tog, k to end.
Rep this row until 3 sts rem.
Sl1 k2tog psso.
Bind (cast) off.

FOR THE PUPPY HEAD

Work from back of head to front.
Using US size 6 (4mm) double-pointed needles and leaving a long tail, cast on 5 sts.
Round 1: Kfb in each st to end, join into round, place marker. *10 sts.*
Round 2: K.
Round 3: Kfb in each st to end. *20 sts.*
Round 4: K.
Round 5: [K1, kfb] to end. *30 sts.*
Rounds 6–8: K.
Round 9: [K2, kfb] to end. *40 sts.*
Rounds 10–14: K.
Round 15: K10, [k2tog] 10 times, k10. *30 sts.*
Rounds 16–19: K to end, on Round 19 place marker between sts 15 and 16 to mark center of face.
Round 20: K.
Cut separate strand of yarn, approx. 18in (46cm) long in same color, thread through each st of round at back of work, leaving 2 long ends for gathering later.
Rounds 21–24: K.
Round 25: [K1, k2tog] to end. *20 sts.*
Round 26: K.
Round 27: [K2tog] around. *10 sts.*
Stuff muzzle.
Cut yarn leaving long tail, thread yarn tail onto yarn sewing needle and thread through rem 10 sts. Pull tight to gather and sew in end.
Thread cast-on end onto yarn sewing needle, sew around cast-on sts, pull tight and sew in end.
Pull the two ends prev threaded round stitches of Round 20, make a knot to secure, and sew in ends. This gathers in to form muzzle shape.

tip
Make the heads in between making the mini blankets, when the yarn colors finish on either pale pink (rabbit), bright pink (teddy), or lilac (puppy). Use either the outside end or the inside end of the yarn, depending on the colors preferred.

FOR THE PUPPY EARS

(make 2)
Using US size 6 (4mm) double-pointed needles and leaving a long tail, cast on 8 sts.
Join into round, place marker.
Rounds 1–2: K.
Round 3: K1, [M1, k1] twice, k2, [k1, M1] twice, k1.
12 sts.
Round 4: K.
Round 5: K1, [M1, k1] 3 times, k4, [k1, M1] 3 times, k1.
18 sts.

Rounds 6–13: K.
Round 14: K1, [k2tog] 3 times, k4, [k2tog] 3 times, k1.
12 sts.
Round 15: [K2tog] 6 times. *6 sts.*
Cut yarn leaving long tail, thread yarn tail onto yarn sewing needle and thread through rem 6 sts. Pull tight and sew in end.

FOR THE TEDDY HEAD

Work from back of head to front.
Using US size 6 (4mm) double-pointed needles and leaving a long tail, cast on 5 sts.
Round 1: Kfb in each st to end, join round, place marker. *10 sts.*
Round 2: K.
Round 3: Kfb in each st to end. *20 sts.*
Round 4: K.
Round 5: [K1, kfb] to end. *30 sts.*
Rounds 6–8: K.
Round 9: [K2, kfb] to end. *40 sts.*
Rounds 10–12: K.
Round 13: K10, [k2tog] 10 times, k10. *30 sts.*
Rounds 14–15: K to end, on Round 15 place marker between sts 15 and 16 to mark center of face.
Round 16: K.
Cut separate strand of yarn, approx. 18in (46cm) long in same color, thread through each st of round at back of work, leaving 2 long ends for gathering later.
Rounds 17–20: K.
Round 21: [K1, k2tog] to end. *20 sts.*
Round 22: K.
Round 23: [K2tog] around. *10 sts.*
Stuff muzzle.
Cut yarn leaving long tail, thread yarn tail onto yarn sewing needle and thread through rem 10 sts. Pull tight to gather and sew in end.
Thread cast-on end onto yarn sewing needle, sew around cast-on stitches, pull tight and sew in end.
Pull the two ends prev threaded round stitches of Round 15, make a knot to secure, and sew in ends. This gathers in to form the muzzle shape.

FOR THE TEDDY EARS

(make 2)
Using US size 6 (4mm) double-pointed needles, cast on 6 sts, join round, place marker.
Round 1: Kfb in each st around. *12 sts.*
Rounds 2–5: K.
Bind (cast) off, leaving a long tail.

FOR THE BUNNY HEAD

Starting at back of head.
Using US size 6 (4mm) needles, cast on 7 sts.
Row 1: K1, [kfb, k1] 3 times. *10 sts.*
Row 2: P.
Row 3: K2, [kfb, k1] 4 times. *14 sts.*
Row 4: P.
Row 5: K2, [kfb, k2] 4 times. *18 sts.*
Row 6: P.
Row 7: K2, [kfb, k1] 8 times. *26 sts.*
Starting with a p row, work st st for 10 rows.
Row 18: P3, [p2tog, p1] 6 times, p2tog, p3. *19 sts.*
Row 19: K.
Row 20: P4, [p2tog, p1] 3 times, p2tog, p4. *15 sts.*
Row 21: K.
Row 22: P4, p2tog, p3, p2tog, p4. *13 sts.*
Row 23: K.
Row 24: P.
Row 25: K.
Row 26: [P2tog] 6 times, p1. *7 sts.*
Cut yarn, leaving long end. Stuff head. Thread yarn end onto yarn sewing needle, thread through rem sts, gather tightly and sew in end.
With RS together, sew along bottom seam, leaving gap for stuffing. Turn RS out and stuff firmly. Sew up gap.

FOR THE BUNNY EARS

(make 2)
Starting at base of ear.
Using US size 6 (4mm) needles, cast on 5 sts.
Rows 1 and 2: K.
Row 3: K1, [kfb] 3 times, k1. *8 sts.*
Rows 4–16: K.
Row 17: K1, k2tog, k2, k2tog, k1. *6 sts.*
Row 18: K.
Row 19: K1, [k2tog] twice, k1. *4 sts.*
Row 20: K.
Row 21: K2tog, k1. *3 sts.*
Cut yarn, thread through rem sts, gather tightly and sew in end.

FINISHING

Block blankies and sew in any yarn ends.

Using the photo on page 96 as a guide, embroider the face details on each head.
Sew the matching ears to each head.

Sew each animal head to the RS of one corner of a blankie, by attaching the tip of the corner to the back of the animal head that matches the color of the blankie.

MATERIALS

Caron Cakes (100% acrylic, approx. 382yds/350m per 7oz/200g ball) worsted (aran) weight yarn
  2 balls of 17023 Rainbow Sherbet

US size 10 (6mm) knitting needles

Yarn sewing needle

2yd (2m) fleece lining fabric

Sewing needle and thread

5 buttons

5 snap fasteners

FINISHED MEASUREMENTS

To fit 0–3 month old baby

One size approx. 17¾in (45cm) wide x 27½in (70cm) long

GAUGE (TENSION)

14½ sts x 28 rows over a 4in (10cm) square in garter stitch, using US size 10 (6mm) needles.

ABBREVIATIONS

approx.	approximately
beg	beginning
k	knit
LH	left hand
rem	remain(ing)
rep	repeat
RH	right hand
RS	right side
sl	slip
st(s)	stitch(es)
WS	wrong side

baby's sleeping bag

Worked in a zingy bright yarn with a lovely fleecy lining, this makes a cozy sleeping bag for a little one.

FOR THE BACK AND HOOD

Cast on 66 sts.
Work in garter st (every row k) until work measures approx. 27½in (70cm).
Bind (cast) off.

FOR THE FRONT

(make 2)
Cast on 36 sts.
Work in garter st (every row k) until work measures approx. 21½in (55cm).
Bind (cast) off.

tip
For a bigger bag, work extra rows to the required length.

FINISHING

Block and sew in any yarn ends.
Using each individual piece as a template, cut a piece of fleece lining to match. Turn under ⅜in (1cm) for the seam allowance and, with WS together, oversew the lining centrally to each piece.

With RS together, place each of the two front rectangles over the back, with the bottom edge aligned and with the front pieces overlapping for the button flap. Oversew the back and fronts together along the outer sides and bottom only.

With RS facing, fold the outer corners at the top of the back into the center to create a triangle that will form the hood. Sew the center hood seam using mattress stitch.

Make a 5in (13cm) long tassel (see page 126). Sew to the point of the hood.

Sew the buttons on the RS evenly along the top flap of the front.

Sew a snap fastener to either side of the overlapping flaps underneath each button.

PICOT EDGING

With WS facing, starting from beg of hood edge, join yarn and pick up 65 sts evenly around hood opening.
Next row: Bind (cast) off 2 sts, *sl rem st on RH needle onto LH needle, cast on 2 sts, bind (cast) off 4 sts; rep from * to end, fasten off rem st.

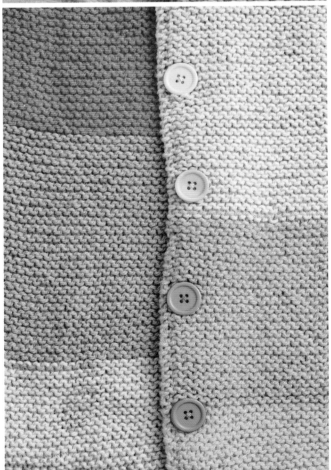

diamonds baby blanket with pompoms

This blanket has really subtle tones and the pompoms are a lovely fun touch.
The diamond brocade stitch gives it a gorgeous traditional look.

SKILL RATING ● ● ●

MATERIALS

Schoppel Wolle Gradient (100% wool,
approx. 284yds/260m per 3½oz/100g
ball) light worsted (DK) weight yarn
  4 balls of 2306 Yellow Filter

Small amounts of orange, pink, yellow,
and green yarn for pompoms

US size 4 (3.5mm) circular needle, 32in
(80cm) long

Yarn sewing needle

2in (5cm) diameter pompom maker

FINISHED MEASUREMENTS

Approx. 34 x 34in (86.5 x 86.5cm)

GAUGE (TENSION)

18½ sts x 31 rows over a 4in (10cm)
square in diamond brocade stitch, using
US size 4 (3.5mm) circular needle.

ABBREVIATIONS

approx.	approximately
foll	following
k	knit
p	purl
patt	pattern
rep	repeat
RS	right side
st(s)	stitch(es)
[ ]	repeat sequence between square brackets the number of times stated

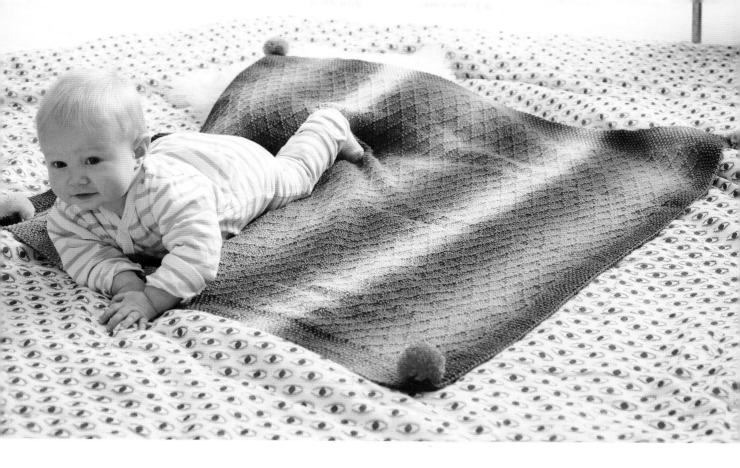

FOR THE BLANKET

Cast on 157 sts.
Work backward and forward in rows.

SEED (MOSS) ST BORDER

Row 1 (RS): [K1, p1] to last st, k1.
Rep this row 13 more times.

START MAIN PATT

Keep seed (moss) st patt as set for first and last 10 sts on each foll row.
Row 1 (RS): [K1, p1] 5 times, k4, [p1, k7] to last 15 sts, p1, k4, [p1, k1] 5 times.
Row 2: [K1, p1] 5 times, p3, *k1, p1, k1, p5; rep from * to last 16 sts, k1, p1, k1, p3, [p1, k1] 5 times.
Row 3: [K1, p1] 5 times, k2, [p1, k3] to last 13 sts, p1, k2, [p1, k1] 5 times.
Row 4: [K1, p1] 5 times, p1, *k1, p5, k1, p1; rep from * to last 10 sts, [p1, k1] 5 times.
Row 5: [K1, p1] 5 times, [p1, k7] to last 11 sts, p1, [p1, k1] 5 times.
Row 6: Rep Row 4.
Row 7: Rep Row 3.
Row 8: Rep Row 2.
These 8 rows form patt, rep them until work measures approx. 33in (84cm) ending on a Row 8.

SEED (MOSS) ST BORDER

Row 1 (RS): [K1, p1] to last st, k1.
Rep this row 13 more times.
Bind (cast) off loosely.

FINISHING

Block and sew in any yarn ends.

Make 4 small pompoms, one in each colour, and attach one to each corner.

cable sweater

Traditional cable sweaters look lovely on babies, and the gradient coloring of this sweater makes it super-interesting to knit.

SKILL RATING ● ● ●

MATERIALS

Schoppel Wolle Gradient (100% wool, approx. 284yds/260m per 3½oz/100g ball) light worsted (DK) weight yarn
1(**2**:2:**2**:3) balls of 2336 Woman in the Woods

US size 6 (4mm) and US size 7 (4.5mm) knitting needles

Set of 5 US size 6 (4mm) double-pointed needles

Cable needle

Stitch holder

Yarn sewing needle

GAUGE (TENSION)

19 sts x 25 rows over a 4in (10cm) square in stockinette (stocking) stitch using US size 7 (4.5mm) needles.

Cable panel 6in (15cm) wide slightly stretched

FINISHED MEASUREMENTS

To fit:		6–12 months	**12–18 months**	18–24 months	**2–3years**	3–4 years
ACTUAL MEASUREMENTS						
Chest:		19	**20**	21½	**22½**	23¼in
		48	**51**	54.5	**57**	59cm
Length to shoulder:		9	**10½**	12¼	**14½**	16½in
		23	**27**	31	**37**	42cm
Sleeve length:		6	**6¾**	8	**9½**	10½in
		15	**17**	20	**24**	27cm

ABBREVIATIONS

approx.	approximately	**M1**	make 1 stitch	**st(s)**	stitch(es)
beg	beginning	**M1p**	make 1 stitch purlwise	**st st**	stockinette (stocking) stitch
cont	continue	**p**	purl	**WS**	wrong side
dec	decrease	**patt**	pattern	**[ ]**	repeat sequence between
foll	following	**rep**	repeat		square brackets the number
inc	increase	**RS**	right side		of times stated
k	knit	**sl**	slip		
k2tog	knit 2 stitches together	**sl1 k1 psso**	slip 1 stitch, knit 1 stitch, pass slipped stitch over		

SPECIAL ABBREVIATIONS

C2B: cable 2 back: sl next st on to cable needle, and hold to back, k1, k1 from cable needle

C2F: cable 2 front: sl next st on to cable needle, and hold to front, k1, k1 from cable needle

C4B: cable 4 back: sl next 2 sts on to cable needle, and hold to back, k2, k2 from cable needle

C4F: cable 4 front: sl next 2 sts on to cable needle, and hold to front, k2, k2 from cable needle

C6B: cable 6 back: sl next 3 sts on to cable needle, and hold to back, k3, k3 from cable needle

Tw4B: twist 4 back: sl next st on to cable needle, and hold to back, k3, p1 from cable needle

Tw4F: twist 4 front: sl next 3 sts on to cable needle, and hold to front, p1, k3 from cable needle

FOR THE BACK

Using US size 6 (4mm) needles, cast on
48(**50**:54:**56**:58) sts.
Row 1: [K1, p1] to end.
Rep Row 1 until work measures
1¼(**1¼**:1¼:**1½**:1½)in/3(**3**:3:**4**:4)cm.
Change to US size 7 (4.5mm) needles.
Set-up row (WS): P9(**10**:12:**13**:14), k1, M1p, p1,
k3, p1, M1p, p2, k3, p1 M1p, p1, k4, p1 M1p,
p1, k3, p2, M1p, p1, k3, p1, M1p, k1, p to end.
*54(**56**:60:**62**:64) sts.*

BEG CABLE PATT

Row 1: K9(**10**:12:**13**:14), p1, k2, p3, k4, p3,
Tw4F, p2, Tw4B, p3, k4, p3, k2, p1, k to end.
Row 2: P9(**10**:12:**13**:14), k1, p2, k3, p4, k4, p3,
k2, p3, k4, p4, k3, p2, k1, p to end.
Row 3: K9(**10**:12:**13**:14), p1, C2B, p3, C4B, p4,
Tw4F, Tw4B, p4, C4F, p3, C2F, p1, k to end.
Row 4: P9(**10**:12:**13**:14), k1, p2, k3, p4, k5, p6,
k5, p4, k3, p2, k1, p to end.

Row 5: K9(**10**:12:**13**:14), p1, k2, p3, k4, p5, C6B, p5, k4, p3, k2, p1, k to end.
Row 6: Rep Row 4.
Row 7: K9(**10**:12:**13**:14), p1, C2B, p3, k4, p4, Tw4B, Tw4F, p4, k4, p3, C2F, p1, k to end.
Row 8: Rep Row 2.
Row 9: K9(**10**:12:**13**:14), p1, k2, p3, C4B, p3, Tw4B, p2, Tw4F, p3, C4F, p3, k2, p1, k to end.
Row 10: P9(**10**:12:**13**:14), k1, p2, k3, p4, k3, p3, k4, p3, k3, p4, k3, p2, k1, p to end.
Row 11: K9(**10**:12:**13**:14), p1, C2B, p3, k4, p3, k3, p4, k3, p3, k4, p3, C2F, p1, k to end.
Row 12: Rep Row 10.
Rep Rows 1–12 for rest of back.**
Cont straight until back measures 9(**10½**:12¼:**14½**:16½) in/23(**27**:31:**37**:42)cm from cast on, ending with a WS row.
Bind (cast) off.

FOR THE FRONT

Work as back to **.
Cont straight until front measures 6¾(**8¼**:9½:**11½**:13½) in/17(**21**:24:**29**:34)cm from cast on, ending with a WS row.

SHAPE NECK

Next row: Patt 21(**22**:23:**24**:25), bind (cast) off 12(**12**:14:**14**:14) sts, patt to end.
Cont on right shoulder sts only.
Next row: Patt to end.
Next row: Sl1 k1 psso, patt to end. *20(21:22:23:24) sts.*
Cont to dec at neck edge on foll 3(**3**:2:**3**:3) RS rows and then on foll 1(**1**:2:**2**:2) 4th rows. *16(17:18:18:19) sts.*
Cont straight until front matches back to shoulder, ending with a WS row.
Bind (cast) off.
With WS facing, rejoin yarn to left shoulder and patt to end.
Next row: Patt to last two sts, k2tog. *20(21:22:23:24) sts.*
Cont to dec at neck edge on foll 3(**3**:2:**3**:3) RS rows and then on foll 1(**1**:2:**2**:2) 4th rows. *16(17:18:18:19) sts.*
Cont straight until front matches back to start of rib, ending with a WS row.
Bind (cast) off.

FOR THE SLEEVES

Using US size 6 (4mm) needles, cast on 29(**29**:31:**33**:33) sts.
Row 1: [K1, p1] to last st, k1.
Row 2: [P1, k1] to last st, p1.
Rep Rows 1 and 2 twice more.
Change to US size 7 (4.5mm) needles and cont in st st, starting with a k row.
Work straight for 2(**2**:2:**6**:6) rows.
Next row: K1, M1, k to last st, M1, k1. *31(**31**:33:**35**:35) sts.*
Cont to inc as set on every RS row to 43(**47**:51:**53**:49) sts and then on every 4th row to –(**–**:–:**55**:59) sts.
Work straight to 6(**6¾**:8:**9½**:10½)in/15(**17**:20:**24**:27)cm.
Bind (cast) off.

FOR THE NECKBAND

Join shoulder seams.
With RS facing, using US size 6 (4mm) double-pointed needles, pick up and k 11(**11**:13:**15**:15) sts down left neck, 12(**12**:14:**14**:14) sts across front neck bind (cast) off, 11(**11**:13:**15**:15) sts up right front neck and 22(**22**:24:**26**:26) sts across back neck. *56(**56**:64:**70**:70) sts.*

Round 1: [K1, p1] to end.
Work 5 more rounds in rib.
Bind (cast) off in rib.

FINISHING

Block and sew in any yarn ends.

Mark side seams 4¼(**4¾**:5:**5½**:6)in/11(**12**:13:**14**:15)cm down from shoulders on both sides of front and back. Sew sleeve top evenly to body between markers.

Join sleeve and side seams.

MATERIALS

Schoppel Wolle Gradient (100% wool, approx. 284yds/260m per 3½oz/100g ball) light worsted (DK) weight yarn
  1 ball of 1508 Shadows (A)

Debbie Bliss Baby Cashmerino (55% wool, 33% acrylic, 12% cashmere, approx. 137yds/125m per 1¾oz/50g ball) sport (light DK) weight yarn
  1 ball of 78 Lipstick Pink (B)

Set of 4 US size 6 (4mm) double-pointed needles

US size 4 (3.5mm) knitting needles

8 stitch markers

Yarn sewing needle

FINISHED MEASUREMENTS

To fit age approx. 4–24 months

Approx. 15in (38cm) circumference, 6½in (16.5cm) high with edge rolled

GAUGE (TENSION)

21 sts x 28 rows over a 4in (10cm) square in stockinette (stocking) stitch, using US size 6 (4mm) needles and Gradient.

ABBREVIATIONS

approx.	approximately
beg	beginning
dec	decrease
k	knit
k2tog	knit 2 stitches together
k3tog	knit 3 stitches together
p	purl
p2tog	purl 2 stitches together
rem	remain
rep	repeat
RS	right side
st st	stockinette (stocking) stitch
st(s)	stitch(es)

bunny baby hat

This is a super-cute hat for a baby—the little bunny ears do wobble about a bit, but that just makes it even more appealing.

FOR THE HAT

Using US size 6 (4mm) double-pointed needles and A, cast on 80 sts equally over 3 needles. Place marker to indicate beg of round.
K until work measures approx. 6in (15cm)—bottom edge of hat will roll up.
Next round: *K10, place marker; rep from * to last 10 sts, k10. *8 st markers.*

BEGIN DEC
*K to 2 sts before marker, k2tog; rep from * until 8 sts rem.
Cut yarn, thread end into yarn sewing needle and draw through rem 8 sts.

FOR THE EARS

(make 4)
Using US size 4 (3.5mm) needles and B, cast on 13 sts.
Rows 1–17: Work in st st, beg with a k row.
Row 12: P2tog, p to last two sts, p2tog.
Row 13: K.
Rep last two rows until 3 sts rem.
Next row: K3tog.
Fasten off.

FINISHING

Block and sew in any yarn ends.

Place two ear pieces RS together and sew around the sides and top, leaving the bottom open. Rep with the other two ear pieces.

Make a running stitch along the bottom of the ears and gather. Using the photo above left as a guide, pin the ears at the top of the hat and sew in place.

sweater dress

This A-line dress is the perfect style for a baby or toddler, and the very simple shaping makes it a real joy to knit. The pompom embellishment on the front gives it an extra cuteness factor!

MATERIALS

Caron Cupcakes (100% acrylic, approx. 243yds/223m per 3oz/85g ball) light worsted (DK) weight yarn 2(**2**:3:**3**:3) balls of 16006 Sweet Berries

US size 5 (3.75mm) and US size 6 (4mm) knitting needles

3 stitch holders

Yarn sewing needle

Stitch markers

4 buttons

1½in (4cm) diameter pompom maker

GAUGE (TENSION)

19 sts x 27 rows over a 4in (10cm) square in stockinette (stocking) stitch, using US size 6 (4mm) needles.

FINISHED MEASUREMENTS

To fit:	6–12 months	**12–18 months**	18–24 months	**2–3 years**	3–4 years
ACTUAL MEASUREMENTS					
Chest:	18¾	**20¼**	21	**22**	23¼in
	47.5	**51.5**	53.5	**56**	60cm
Length to shoulder:	14¼	**15**	16¼	**17½**	18½in
	36	**38**	41	**44**	47cm
Sleeve length:	6¾	**7½**	8¾	**10¼**	11½in
	17	**19**	22	**26**	29cm

ABBREVIATIONS

approx.	approximately	**M1**	make 1 stitch	**st(s)**	stitch(es)
cont	continue	**p**	purl	**st st**	stockinette (stocking) stitch
dec	decrease	**patt**	pattern	**WS**	wrong side
foll	following	**rem**	remain	**yo**	yarn over
inc	increase	**rep**	repeat	**[ ]**	repeat sequence between
k	knit	**RS**	right side		square brackets the number
k2tog	knit 2 stitches together	**sl1 k1 psso**	slip 1 stitch, knit 1 stitch, pass slipped stitch over		of times stated

FOR THE BACK

Using US size 6 (4mm) needles, cast on
77(**79**:81:**83**:85) sts.

SEED (MOSS) ST BORDER
Row 1: [K1, p1] to last st, k1.
Rep this row 3(**3**:5:**5**:5) more times.

BEG PATT ROWS
Cont in st st starting with a k row.
Work straight for 2(**6**:6:**4**:6) rows.
Next row: K1, sl1 k1 psso, k to last 3 sts, k2tog, k1.
*75(**77**:79:**81**:83) sts*.
Cont to dec at each end of every 6th row to
73(**73**:71:**65**:61) sts and then on every 4th row
13(**11**:9:**5**:1) times. *47(**51**:53:**55**:59) sts.* **
Cont straight until back measures
13¾(**14½**:15¾:**17**:18)in/35(**37**:40:**43**:46)cm from
cast-on edge, ending with WS row.
Change to US size 5 (3.75mm) needles.

START RIB BAND
Row 1: [K1, p1] to last st, k1.
Row 2: [P1, k1] to last st, p1.
Rep Rows 1 and 2 twice more.
Bind (cast) off in rib.

FOR THE FRONT

Work as back to **.
Cont straight until front is 10(**10**:12:**12**:16) rows shorter
than back to end of st st section, ending with WS row.

SHAPE NECK
Next row: K18(**19**:20:**20**:22) sts and leave on holder,
bind (cast) off 11(**13**:13:**15**:15) sts, k to end.

RIGHT SHOULDER

Work on rem sts on needle only.
Next row: P to end.
Next row: Sl1 k1 psso, k to end. *17(18:19:19:21) sts.*
Cont to dec as set on foll 6th(**6th**:4th:**4th**:4th) rows
1(**1**:2:**2**:3) times. *16(17:17:17:18) sts.*
Work 1 row.
Leave rem sts on holder.

LEFT SHOULDER

With WS facing, rejoin yarn to left shoulder and p to
end.
Next row: K to last 2 sts, k2tog.
Cont to dec as set on foll 6th(**6th**:4th:**4th**:4th) rows
1(**1**:2:**2**:3) times. *16(17:17:17:18) sts.*
Work 1 row.
Leave rem sts on holder.

FOR THE SLEEVES

Using US size 5 (3.75mm) needles cast on
29(**29**:31:**33**:33) sts.
Row 1: [K1, p1] rib to last st, k1.
Row 2: [P1, k1] to last st, p1.
Rep Rows 1 and 2 twice more.
Change to US size 6 (4mm) needles and cont in st st
starting with a k row.
Work straight for 4(**2**:4:**4**:4) rows.
Next row: K1, M1, k to last st, M1, k1.
31(31:33:35:35) sts.
Cont to inc as set on every foll 4th row to
41(**45**:47:**47**:49) sts and then on every 6th row to
43(**47**:51:**55**:59) sts.
Work straight until work measures
6¾(**7½**:8¾:**10¼**:11½)in/17(**19**:22:**26**:29)cm, ending on
a p row.
Bind (cast) off.

FOR THE FRONT NECKBAND

With RS facing and using US size 5 (3.75mm) needles,
pick up and knit 6(**6**:10:**10**:13) sts down left neck,
11(**13**:13:**15**:15) sts across front neck bind (cast) off,
and 6(**6**:10:**10**:13) sts up left right front neck.
23(25:33:35:41) sts.
Row 1 (WS): [P1, k1] rib to last st, p1.
Row 2: [K1, p1] to last st, k1.
Work 3 more rows in rib.
Bind (cast) off in rib.

FOR THE LEFT FRONT SHOULDER

Return left shoulder sts to US size 5 (3.75mm) needle, with
RS facing k across sts, pick up and k 3(**4**:4:**4**:3) sts along
edge of neckband. *19(21:21:21:21) sts.*
Row 1 (WS): P2, [k1, p1] to last st, k1.
Row 2: [P1, k1] to last 3 sts, p1, k2,
Row 3 (buttonholes): P2, k1, yo, k2tog, rib 6(**7**:7:**7**:7), yo,
k2tog, rib to end.
Work 2 more rows in rib.
Bind (cast) off in rib.

FOR THE RIGHT FRONT SHOULDER

Return right shoulder sts to US size 5 (3.75mm) needle,
with RS facing pick up and k 3(**4**:4:**4**:3) sts along edge of
neckband, k across shoulder sts. *19(21:21:21:21) sts.*
Row 1 (WS): [K1, p1] rib to last 3 sts, k1, p2.
Row 2: K2, p1, [k1, p1] to end.
Row 3 (buttonholes): Rib 7(**8**:8:**8**:8), yo, k2tog, rib
6(**7**:7:**8**:7), yo, k2tog, p2.
Work 2 more rows in rib.
Bind (cast) off in rib.

FINISHING

With RS facing, overlap shoulder ribs with buttonhole
bands on top and pin in place.

Place pin markers on both side seams 4(**4¼**:4¾:**5**:5½)in/
10(**11**:12:**13**:14)cm down from the start of the rib on both
front and back. Fold the sleeve in half lengthwise with RS
together and place a pin marker on the center fold, at the
top. With RS together, match the marker pin on the sleeve
with the middle row of the buttonband rib at the armhole
edge and pin the sleeve to the body with the edges of the
sleeve matching the body pin markers. Sew the sleeve top
evenly to the body, easing the stitches between the
markers, and attaching the sleeve to both layers of rib at
the shoulder. Repeat for the other sleeve.

Join the sleeve and side seams.

Block and sew in any yarn ends. Attach the buttons to the
shoulders to match the buttonholes.

Each ball of Caron Cupcakes comes with a pompom, so
you can use these if you have enough, or make 3 small
pompoms (see page 126) if you prefer. Sew the pompoms
in a line evenly spaced out down the front of the dress.

techniques

Gauge (tension)

A gauge (tension) is given with each pattern to help you make your item the same size as the sample. The gauge is given as the number of stitches and rows you need to work to produce a 4in (10cm) square of knitting.

Using the recommended yarn and needles, cast on 8 stitches more than the gauge instruction asks for, so if you need to have 10 stitches to 4in (10cm), cast on 18 stitches. Working in pattern as instructed, work eight rows more than is needed. Bind (cast) off loosely.

Lay the swatch flat without stretching it. Lay a ruler across the stitches as shown, with the 2in (5cm) mark centered on the knitting, then put a pin in the knitting at the start of the ruler and at the 4in (10cm) mark: the pins should be well away from the edges of the swatch. Count the number of stitches between the pins. Repeat the process across the rows to count the number of rows to 4in (10cm).

If the number of stitches and rows you've counted is the same as the number asked for in the instructions, you have the correct gauge. If you do not have the same number then you will need to adjust your gauge.

To adjust gauge you need to change the size of your knitting needles—use larger needles to achieve fewer stitches and smaller ones to achieve more stitches.

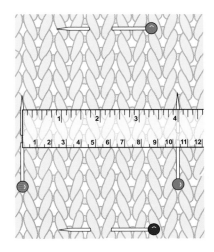

Holding needles

If you are a knitting novice, you will need to discover which is the most comfortable way for you to hold your needles.

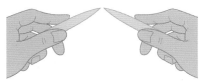

Like a knife

Pick up the needles, one in each hand, as if you were holding a knife and fork—that is to say, with your hands lightly over the top of each needle. As you knit, you will tuck the blunt end of the right-hand needle under your arm, let go with your hand, and use your hand to manipulate the yarn, returning your hand to the needle to move the stitches along.

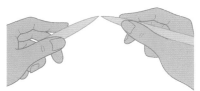

Like a pen

Now try changing the right hand so you are holding the needle as you would hold a pen, with your thumb and forefinger lightly gripping the needle close to its pointed tip and the shaft resting in the crook of your thumb. As you knit, you will not need to let go of the needle but simply slide your right hand forward to manipulate the yarn.

Holding yarn

As you knit, you will be working stitches off the left-hand needle and onto the right-hand needle, and the yarn you are working with needs to be tensioned and manipulated to produce an even fabric. To hold and tension the yarn you can use either your right or left hand, depending on the method you are going to use to make the stitches.

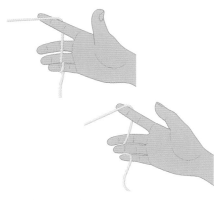

Yarn in right hand

To knit and purl in the American/British style (see pages 116 and 117), hold the yarn in your right hand. You can wind the yarn around your fingers in different ways, depending on how tightly you need to hold it to achieve an even gauge (tension). Try both ways shown to find out which works best for you.

To hold the yarn tightly (top), wind it right around your little finger, under your ring and middle fingers, then pass it over your index finger, which will manipulate the yarn.

For a looser hold (bottom), catch the yarn between your little and ring fingers, pass it under your middle finger, then over your index finger.

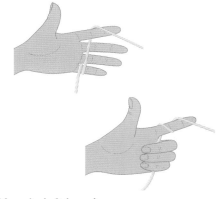

Yarn in left hand

To knit and purl in the continental style (see pages 116 and 117), hold the yarn in your left hand. This method is sometimes easier for left-handed people to use, though many left-handers are quite comfortable knitting with the yarn in their right hand. Try the ways shown to find out which works best for you.

To hold the yarn tightly (top), wind it right around your little finger, under your ring and middle fingers, then pass it over your index finger, which will manipulate the yarn.

For a looser hold (bottom), fold your little, ring, and middle fingers over the yarn, and wind it twice around your index finger.

Making a slipknot

You need to make a slipknot to form the first cast-on stitch.

1 With the ball of yarn on your right, lay the end of the yarn on the palm of your left hand and hold it in place with your left thumb. With your right hand, take the yarn around your top two fingers to form a loop. Take the knitting needle through the back of the loop from right to left and use it to pick up the strand nearest to the yarn ball, as shown in the diagram. Pull the strand through to form a loop at the front.

2 Slip the yarn off your fingers, leaving the loop on the needle. Gently pull on both yarn ends to tighten the knot. Then pull on the yarn leading to the ball of yarn to tighten the knot on the needle.

Casting on (cable method)

There are a few methods of casting on for various shawl projects and this one, the cable method, uses two needles.

1 Make a slipknot as shown above. Put the needle with the slipknot into your left hand. Insert the point of the other needle into the front of the slipknot and under the left-hand needle. Wind the yarn from the ball of yarn around the tip of the right-hand needle.

2 Using the tip of the needle, draw the yarn through the slipknot to form a loop. This loop is the new stitch. Slip the loop from the right-hand needle onto the left-hand needle.

3 To make the next stitch, insert the tip of the right-hand needle between the two stitches. Wind the yarn over the right-hand needle, from left to right, then draw the yarn through to form a loop. Transfer this loop to the left-hand needle. Repeat until you have cast on the right number of stitches for the project.

Binding (casting) off

You need to bind (cast) off the stitches to complete a project and prevent the knitting from unraveling.

1 First knit two stitches in the usual way. With the point of the left-hand needle, pick up the first stitch you have just knitted and lift it over the second stitch. Knit another stitch so that there are two stitches on the right-hand needle again. Repeat the process of lifting the first stitch over the second stitch. Continue this process until just one stitch remains on the right-hand needle.

2 Break the yarn, leaving a tail of yarn long enough to sew the work together (see page 124). Pull the tail all the way through the last stitch. Slip the stitch off the needle and pull it fairly tightly to make sure it is secure.

Knit stitch

There are only two stitches to master in knitting; knit and purl. Likewise, there are two main styles of knitting (with a sprinkling of other international techniques); the American/British style and a method referred to as Continental style.

American/British style

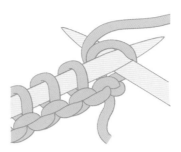  

1 Hold the needle with the cast-on stitches in your left hand, and then insert the point of the right-hand needle into the front of the first stitch from left to right. Wind the yarn around the point of the right-hand needle, from left to right.

2 With the tip of the right-hand needle, pull the yarn through the stitch to form a loop. This loop is the new stitch.

3 Slip the original stitch off the left-hand needle by gently pulling the right-hand needle to the right. Repeat these steps until you have knitted all the stitches on the left-hand needle. To work the next row, transfer the needle with all the stitches into your left hand.

Continental style

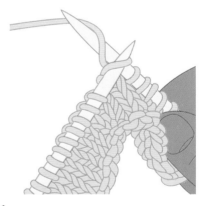 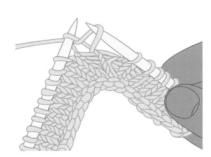 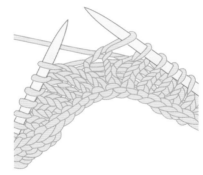

1 Hold the needle with the stitches to be knitted in your left hand, and then insert the tip of the right-hand needle into the front of the first stitch from left to right. Holding the yarn fairly taut with your left hand at the back of your work, use the tip of the right-hand needle to pick up a loop of yarn.

2 With the tip of the right-hand needle, bring the yarn through the original stitch to form a loop. This loop is the new stitch.

3 Slip the original stitch off the left-hand needle by gently pulling the right-hand needle to the right. Repeat these steps until you have knitted all the stitches on the left-hand needle. To work the next row, transfer the needle with all the stitches into your left hand.

Purl stitch

As with knit stitch, purl stitch can be formed in two ways. If you are new to knitting, try both techniques to see which works better for you: left-handed knitters may find the Continental method easier to master.

American/British style

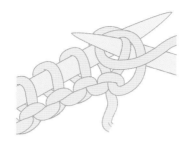

1 Hold the needle with the stitches in your left hand, and then insert the point of the right-hand needle into the front of the first stitch from right to left. Wind the yarn around the point of the right-hand needle, from right to left.

2 With the tip of the right-hand needle, pull the yarn through the stitch to form a loop. This loop is the new stitch.

3 Slip the original stitch off the left-hand needle by gently pulling the right-hand needle to the right. Repeat these steps until you have purled all the stitches on the left-hand needle. To work the next row, transfer the needle with all the stitches into your left hand.

Continental style

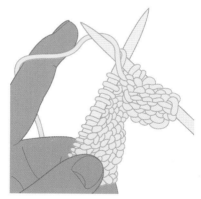

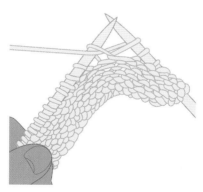

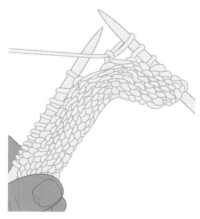

1 Hold the needle with the stitches to be knitted in your left hand, and then insert the tip of the right-hand needle into the front of the first stitch from right to left. Holding the yarn fairly taut at the front of the work, move the tip of the right-hand needle under the working yarn, then push your left index finger downward, as shown, to hold the yarn around the needle.

2 With the tip of the right-hand needle, bring the yarn through the original stitch to form a loop.

3 Slip the original stitch off the left-hand needle by gently pulling the right-hand needle to the right. Repeat these steps until you have purled all the stitches on the left-hand needle. To work the next row, transfer the needle with all the stitches into your left hand.

Bobble stitch

A bobble is created by increasing several times into the same stitch, then decreasing in the following row.

By increasing just once into a stitch, then decreasing in the following row, you will create a tiny indent of texture. Increasing more than once into the same stitch produces a larger physical area for the bobble. You can widen the increased area to include two or more stitches, before decreasing, which will create a defined ridge or bobble.

Loop stitch

Insert right needle into loop on left needle as if to knit st as normal. Wrap yarn around needle and bring right needle through as if knitting st, but do not slip loop off needle. Open out needles, keeping right thumb in middle, bring yarn over to front wrapping

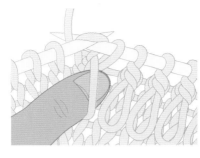

it round thumb, pass the yarn through to back between needles (yarn is wrapped around thumb). Knit st with thumb still wrapped by yarn. Release thumb from strand of yarn to create loop. Slip first st over second to secure loop (one loop stitch made).

Cables

Cables involve moving groups of stitches, and you will need a cable needle to hold the stitches being moved. Work a six-stitch cable as shown here: if it is a four stitch cable, then slip two stitches onto the needle and knit two, rather than three. For an eight-stitch cable, slip four stitches onto the needle and knit four.

Working a six-stitch front cable

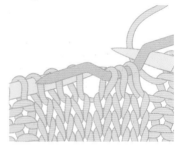
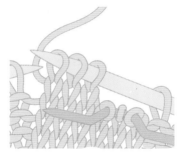
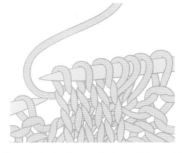

1 Work to the position of the cable. Slip the next three stitches on the left-hand needle onto the cable needle, keeping the cable needle in front of the work. Leave the three stitches on the cable needle in the middle so they don't slip off.

2 Knit the next three stitches off the left-hand needle in the usual way.

3 Then knit the three stitches off the cable needle and the cable is completed.

Working a six-stitch back cable

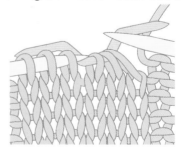

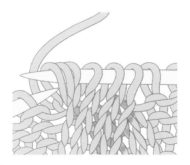

1 Work to the position of the cable. Slip the next three stitches on the left-hand needle onto the cable needle, keeping the cable needle at the back of the work. Leave the three stitches in the middle of the cable needle so they don't slip off.

2 Knit the next three stitches off the left-hand needle in the usual way.

3 Then knit the three stitches off the cable needle and the cable is completed.

Slipping stitches

Knitwise

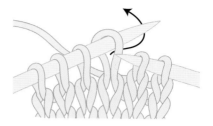

From left to right, put the right-hand needle into the next stitch on the left-hand needle (as shown by the arrow) and slip it across onto the right-hand needle without working it.

Purlwise

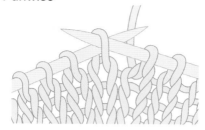

You can slip a stitch purlwise on a purl row or a knit row. From right to left, put the right-hand needle into the next stitch on the left-hand needle and slip it across onto the right-hand needle without working it.

In some cases you will be instructed to bring the yarn to the front of the work before slipping a stitch purlwise.

Yarn over (yo)

To make a yarn over you wind the yarn around the right-hand needle to make an extra loop that is worked as a stitch on the next row.

To make a yarn over between knit stitches (right) bring the yarn between the tips of the needles to the front. Take the yarn over the right-hand needle to the back and knit the next stitch on the left-hand needle (see page 116).

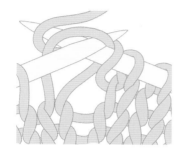

To make a yarn over between purl stitches (above), wrap the yarn over and right around the right-hand needle. Purl the next stitch on the left-hand needle (see page 117).

Increasing

There are two methods of increasing used in this book.

Knit front and back (kfb)

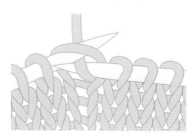

1 Knit the next stitch on the left-hand needle in the usual way (see page 116), but do not slip the "old" stitch off the left-hand needle.

2 Move the right-hand needle behind the left-hand needle and put it into the same stitch again, but through the back of the stitch this time. Knit the stitch again.

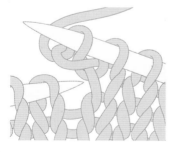

3 Now slip the "old" stitch off the left-hand needle in the usual way.

Make 1 (M1)

Pick up the horizontal strand between two stitches with your left-hand needle from front to back. Knit into the back of the loop, transferring the stitch to the right-hand needle in the normal way. It is important to knit into the back of the loop so that the yarn is twisted and does not form a hole in your work.

Decreasing

There are several ways of decreasing used in this book, some of which decrease by two or more stitches rather than one stitch.

Knit two together (k2tog)

This is the simplest way of decreasing. Simply insert the right-hand needle through two stitches instead of the normal one, and then knit them in the usual way.

The same principle is used to knit three stitches together (k3tog): just insert the right-hand needle through three stitches instead of through two.

Purl two together (p2tog)

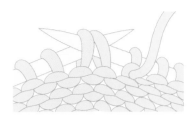

To make a simple decrease on a purl row, insert the right-hand needle through two stitches instead of the normal one, and then purl them in the usual way.

The same principle is used to purl three stitches together (p3tog): just insert the right-hand needle through three stitches instead of through two.

Slip, slip, knit (ssk)

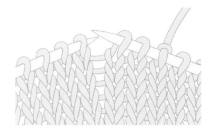

1 Slip one stitch knitwise, and then the next stitch knitwise onto the right-hand needle, without knitting them.

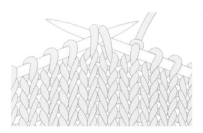

2 Insert the left-hand needle from left to right through the front loops of both the slipped stitches and knit them in the usual way.

Slip 1, knit 1 stitch, pass the slipped stitch over (sl1 k1 psso)

Slip the first stitch knitwise from the left needle to the right needle without knitting it (see page 119). Knit the next stitch, then lift the slipped stitch over the knitted stitch and drop it off the needle.

Slip 2 stitches together knitwise, knit 1 stitch, pass the slipped stitches over (sl2tog k1 psso)

Reduce the number of stitches by two using this decrease.

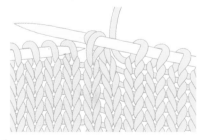

1 Insert the right needle into the next two stitches on the left needle, as if you were about to k2tog (see above). Instead, slip them on to the right needle and do not knit them.

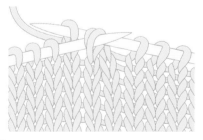

2 Knit the next stitch as normal, then lift the two slipped stitches over the knitted stitch and and drop them off the needle. You have decreased by two stitches.

Knit 2 stitches together through back loops (k2tog tbl)

This is worked in a similar way to k2tog, but instead of inserting the right needle into the stitches from front to back, you insert it from right to left, through the back of the two stitches, and then you knit them together.

Purl 2 stitches together through back loops (p2tog tbl)

Starting at the back of the work, insert the right needle into the back of the next two stitches, from left to right. This will feel counter-intuitive but it is correct; the needle will emerge toward the front. Then purl the two stitches together from this position.

Knitting in the round

You can knit seamless tubes by working round and round rather than back and forth. There are three ways of doing this, depending on how large the tube needs to be. When working in the round you only work knit stitches (see page 116) to create a stockinette (stocking) stitch fabric.

Circular needles

These needles have short straight tips that are joined with a nylon cable. As well as the usual needle size information, the pattern will tell you what length of needle you need so that your stitches fit on it without stretching.

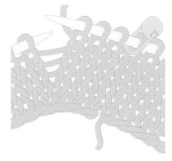

1 Cast on the number of stitches needed (see page 115); just ignore the cable connecting the two tips and cast on the stitches as if you were using two separate needles. Spread out the cast-on row along the length of the cable, making sure the stitches do not become twisted as this will create an unwanted twist in your knitting.

2 Knit the stitches from the right-hand tip onto the left-hand tip, sliding them around the cable as you work. The first stitch is the beginning of the round, so place a round marker on the needle to keep track of the rounds. When you get back to the marker, you have completed one round. Slip the marker onto the right-hand tip of the needle and knit the next round.

Double-pointed needles

If you do not have enough stitches to stretch around a circular needle (see above), then you need to work on double-pointed needles. This is one of those knitting techniques that looks terrifying, but isn't actually that hard to do; you just ignore all the needles other than the two you are working with. Double-pointed needles—usually called "DPNs"—come in sets of four or five and a pattern will tell you how many you need.

1 Divide evenly into three (if using four needles), or into four (if using five needles), the number of stitches you need to cast on. Here, a set of four needles is being used. Cast on (see page 115) to one needle one-third of the number of stitches needed, plus one extra stitch. Slip the extra stitch onto the second needle. Repeat the process, not forgetting to count the extra stitch, until the right number of stitches is cast on to each of the needles.

2 Arrange the needles in a triangle with the tips overlapping as shown here. As with circular needles (see above) make sure that the cast-on edge is not twisted and place a marker to keep track of the beginning of the round. Pull the working tail of yarn across from the last stitch and using the free needle, knit the first stitch off the first needle, knitting it firmly and pulling the yarn tight. Knit the rest of the stitches on the first needle, which then becomes the free one, ready to knit the stitches off the second needle. Knit the stitches off each needle in turn; when you get back to the marker, you have completed one round. Slip the marker onto the next needle and knit the next round.

Picking up stitches

For some projects, you will need to pick up stitches along either the row-end edge or the cast-on/bound- (cast-) off edge of the knitting. The picked-up stitches are shown here in a contrast color for clarity.

Picking up along a row-end edge

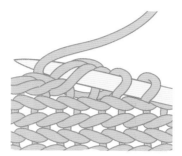

With the right side of the knitting facing you, put a knitting needle from front to back between the first and second stitches of the first row. Wind the yarn around the needle and pull through a loop to form the new stitch. As a knitted stitch is wider than it is tall, you will need to miss out picking up a stitch from about every fourth row in order to make sure the picked-up edge lies flat and even.

Picking up along a cast-on or bound- (cast-) off edge

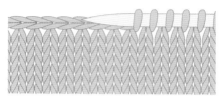

This is worked in the same way as picking up stitches along a vertical edge, except you will work through the cast-on stitches rather than the gaps between rows. You can pick up one stitch from every existing stitch.

Weaving in ends

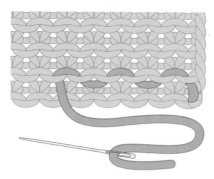

Use a large-eyed knitter's sewing needle (or a tapestry needle), which has a blunt tip to weave the yarn end in and out of a few stitches—the end is shown here in a contrast color for clarity.

Blocking

If, once you have finished the piece of knitting, it doesn't look as smooth and even as you hoped it would, then blocking it can help. You can also use this process to straighten or to re-shape pieces a little if need be. The precise method of blocking you use depends on the fiber the yarn is spun from: the ball band will give you advice on that.

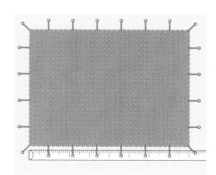

1 Lay the piece of knitting flat on an ironing board and ease it into shape. Don't pull hard and keep the knitting flat. Starting at the corners (if there are any), pin the edges of the piece to the ironing board, pushing the pins in far enough to hold the knitting firmly. Use a ruler or tape measure to check that the pinned pieces are the right size.

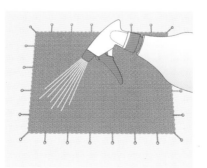

2 If the fiber or texture of your yarn does not respond well to heat, then use a spray bottle of cold water to completely dampen the knitting, but do not make it soaking wet. Let the knitting dry naturally, then unpin it.

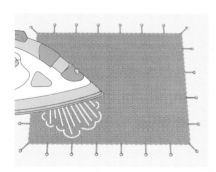

3 If you can use heat, then set the iron to the temperature the yarn ball band recommends. Hold the iron 1in (2.5cm) above the surface of the knitting and steam it for a couple of minutes. Move the iron so that the whole surface gets steamed, but don't actually touch the knitting with the iron as this can spoil the texture and drape of the fabric and may leave shiny patches. Let the knitting dry naturally before unpinning it.

Joining seams

Mattress stitching row-end edges

The seam is worked from the right side and will be almost invisible.

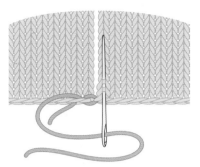

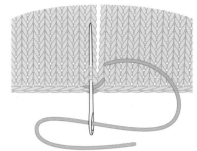

2 Take the needle across to the left-hand piece and, from the front, take it under the bars of yarn between the first and second stitches on the next two rows up.

1 Lay the edges to be joined side by side, right side up. Using a yarn sewing needle threaded with a long length of yarn, bring the needle up between the first and second stitches of the left-hand piece, immediately above the cast-on edge. Take it across to the right-hand piece, and from the back bring it through between the first and second stitches of that piece, immediately above the cast-on edge. Take it back to the left-hand piece and, again from the back, bring it through one row above where it first came through, between the first and second stitches. Pull the yarn through and this figure-eight will hold the cast-on edges level. *Take the needle across to the right-hand piece and, from the front, take it under the bars of yarn between the first and second stitches on the next two rows up.

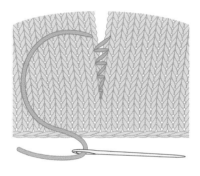

3 Repeat from * to sew up the seam. When you have sewn about 1in (2.5cm), gently and evenly pull the stitches tight to close the seam, and then continue.

Mattress stitching cast-on or bound- (cast-) off edges

You can either gently pull the sewn stitches taut but have them visible, as shown, or you can pull them completely tight so that they disappear.

Oversewing

This stitch can be worked with the right or the wrong sides of the work together.

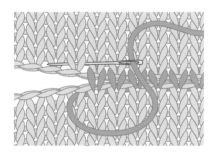

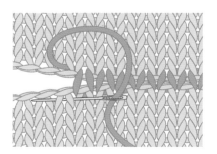

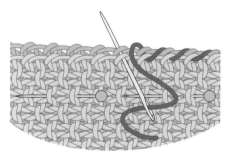

1 Right-sides up, lay the two edges to be joined side by side. Thread a yarn sewing needle with a long length of yarn. Secure the yarn on the back of the lower knitted piece, then bring the needle up through the middle of the first whole stitch in that piece. Take the needle under both loops of the first whole stitch on the upper piece, so that it comes to the front between the first and second stitches.

2 *Go back into the lower piece and take the needle through to the back where it first came out, and then bring it to the front again in the middle of the next stitch along. Pull the yarn through. Take the needle under both loops of the next whole stitch on the upper piece. Repeat from * to sew the seam.

Thread a yarn sewing needle with a tail left after binding (casting) off, or a long length of yarn. Bring the yarn from the back of the work, over the edge of the knitting, and out through to the back again a short distance further on.

Lining a bag

1 Press and block the knitted piece, then measure it. Press the lining to make sure there are no creases. Cut out the fabric lining to fit the knitted piece, allowing an extra 1in (2.5cm) around each edge for hems. For example, if the knitted piece measures 11 x 8½in (28 x 21.5cm), cut out a piece of fabric 13 x 10½in (33 x 26.5cm).

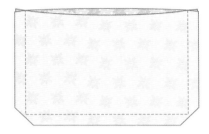

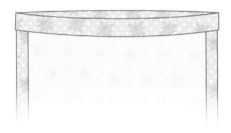

2 Place the two lining pieces with RS together. Pin and sew the side seams, and the bottom seam if there is one, ensuring that the lining is exactly the same measurement, at the sides, as the knitted piece. Trim across the bottom corners. Do not turn RS out.

3 Press the seams open and flat to the WS. Fold the top edge of lining to the outside by 1in (2.5cm) and press in place.

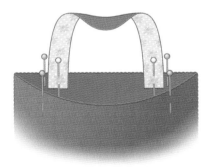

4 Measure the knitted handles and cut out the handle linings the same size plus an extra ⅝ in. (1.5 cm) on each side for the hem. Press the hem to the wrong side along each long edge of the fabric strips. Pin a lining piece, with the hem side down, onto the WS of each knitted handle. Hand sew the lining to the handle using whip stitch. Remove all the pins.

5 Place a pin marker 1 in. (2.5 cm) in from each outside seam along the top edge of the bag, on both front and back. With the knitted side of the handle to the inside of the bag, pin the ends of the first handle to extend down into the bag by about 2 in. (5 cm), with the outer edges to the pin markers. Hand sew the handle to the bag. Repeat to add the second handle on the other side of the bag. Remove any remaining pins.

6 Insert the lining into the bag with WS of knitting and lining together and pin in place around the top edge. Hand sew the lining to the knitted piece around the top edge, stitching across the handles again at the same time for extra security.

Making pompoms

For mini pompoms, you can use the fork method.

  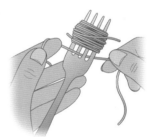

1 Keeping the yarn attached to the ball, wrap it around the prongs of a fork about 20 times. Keep the wraps tight, and center them in the middle of the prongs, leaving space above and below.

2 Cut the yarn and hold the wraps in place on the fork. Cut a 3in (7.5cm) length of yarn and thread it through the middle of the prongs at the bottom from front to back.

3 Wrap one end around and back over the top until the ends meet, then tie them tightly together at the front. Wrap the tie around the center a few more times and tie another knot at the back.

4 Pull the wrap off the fork and pull the knot tighter. The wrap will begin to curl and turn flat and round. Tie another knot on top of the other one to secure. Use sharp embroidering scissors to cut the loops on either side of the tie.

5 Trim the pompom and fluff it up until it's thick and a round, even shape.

Making a tassel

1 Cut a piece of cardboard to the required length for the tassel, to wrap the yarn around. Cut four strands of yarn before you start, three approximately 2½in (6cm) long and another approximately 12in (30cm) long. Wrap the remaining yarn neatly around the cardboard about 25 times.

2 Take the three shorter lengths of yarn, and thread them through all the loops at the top.

3 Hold these pieces as you slide the loops off the cardboard, and then tie them tightly in a double knot.

4 Take the longer length of yarn cut earlier and tie it around the tassel, approx 1in (2.5cm) from the top. Wrap around tightly several times and tie a tight knot. Trim the ends to match the ends of the tassel.

5 Cut the loops at the bottom of the tassel. Braid (plait) together the strands of yarn threaded through the top of the tassel, and tie a double knot at the end of the braid.

suppliers

For reasons of space we cannot cover all stockists, so please explore the local knitting shops and online stores in your own country.

USA

Jo-Ann Fabric and Craft Stores
Retail stores and online sales
www.joann.com

Knitting Fever Inc.
Online sales
www.knittingfever.com

Love Knitting
Online sales
www.loveknitting.com

Maker's Mercantile
Online sales (for Schoppel-Wolle)
www.makersmercantile.com

Michaels
Retail stores and online sales
www.michaels.com

WEBS
Online sales
www.yarn.com

UK

Artyarn
Online sales (for Schoppel-Wolle)
www.artyarn.co.uk

Deramores
Online sales
www.deramores.com

Hobbycraft
Retail stores and online
www.hobbycraft.co.uk

John Lewis
Retail stores and online sales
www.johnlewis.com

Love Knitting
Online sales
www.loveknitting.com

Wool Warehouse
Online sales
www.woolwarehouse.co.uk

AUSTRALIA

Black Sheep Wool 'n' Wares
Retail store and online sales
www.blacksheepwool.com.au

YARN COMPANIES

Bernat and Caron
USA and Canada:
www.spinriteyarns.com
UK and Europe:
www.creativeworldofcrafts.co.uk

James Brett
www.jamescbrett.co.uk

Lion Brand
www.lionbrand.com

Scheepjes
www.scheepjes.com

Schoppel-Wolle
www.schoppel-wolle.de

Sirdar
www.sirdar.co.uk

If you wish to substitute a different yarn for the one recommended in the pattern, try the **Yarnsub** website for suggestions:
www.yarnsub.com

acknowledgments

I have very much enjoyed designing and making the projects for this lovely and exciting book, but I couldn't have done it on my own; I feel very lucky to have so many fantastic people in the background helping and supporting me throughout the time I've been working it.

I would like to say a huge thank you to Cindy Richards for commissioning me; to Penny Craig for doing a fabulous job of project managing; and to designer Alison Fenton, along with Sally Powell and the rest of the team at CICO Books, for putting together such a lovely book. Thank you also to the models (particularly my gorgeous baby granddaughter, Wren Clasen and her mum Camilla Clasen, for a lovely morning taking photos of Wren); and to super-stylist Nel Haynes and fantastic photographer James Gardiner for doing such a great job too.

Thank you also to pattern checkers Jane Czaja and Marilyn Wilson—pattern checking is a very detailed job and you have to be meticulous and super patient. Thanks also to Marie Clayton, who, as always, has made an exceptional job of the editing and checking. I'd also like to say a big thank you to Bronagh Miskelly, who sorts out the grading and sizing for all the garments, and special thanks also to Tina McCara for helping with the patterns and knitting so many of the projects in this book.

Although I make a majority of the projects for photography myself, I also have a really great team of reliable and expert knitters, without whom I would never be able to meet the deadlines. They are Tina McAra, Bronagh Miskelly, Mel Howes, Tracey Elks, Zara Poole, Maggie Hebblesthwaite, Jill Broadhurst, Vikki Haffenden, Anna Hopper, Roberta Couchman, Helen Hadfield, Julie Lanius… and last but not least, my mum, Beryl Oakes—at 89, she is still the same knitter she ever was!

I'm very lucky to have access to some really beautiful yarns and, more than that, some really great suppliers. Particular thanks go to Kirsty Lloyd at Creative World of Crafts (for Bernat and Caron), Schoppel-Wolle, and Scheepjes for providing me with their yarns.

index